This Book Comes With Lots of
FREE Online Resources

Nolo's award-winning website has a page dedicated just to this book. Here you can:

KEEP UP TO DATE. When there are important changes to the information in this book, we'll post updates.

GET DISCOUNTS ON NOLO PRODUCTS. Get discounts on hundreds of books, forms, and software.

READ BLOGS. Get the latest info from Nolo authors' blogs.

LISTEN TO PODCASTS. Listen to authors discuss timely issues on topics that interest you.

WATCH VIDEOS. Get a quick introduction to a legal topic with our short videos.

And that's not all.
Nolo.com contains thousands of articles on everyday legal and business issues, plus a plain-English law dictionary, all written by Nolo experts and available for free. You'll also find more useful **books, software, online apps, downloadable forms,** plus a **lawyer directory.**

With
**Downloadable
FORMS**

Get forms and more at
www.nolo.com/back-of-book/CPOA.html

5th Edition

Living Wills & Powers of Attorney for California

Shae Irving, J.D.

FIFTH EDITION   JANUARY 2017

Book Design   TERRI HEARSH

Proofreading   IRENE BARNARD

Index   VICTORIA BAKER

Printing   BANG PRINTING

Names: Irving, Shae, author.
Title: Living wills & powers of attorney for California / Shae Irving, J.D.
Other titles: Living wills and powers of attorney for California
Description: Fifth Edition. | Berkeley, CA : Nolo, 2017. | Includes index.
Identifiers: LCCN 2016031685 (print) | LCCN 2016031812 (ebook) | ISBN
    9781413323375 (pbk.) | ISBN 9781413323382 (ebook)
Subjects: LCSH: Right to die--Law and legislation--California--Popular works.
    | Do-not-resuscitate--Law and legislation--California--Popular works. |
    Power of attorney--California--Popular works. | Advance directives
    (Medical care)--California.
Classification: LCC KFC619.5.R5 I78 2017 (print) | LCC KFC619.5.R5 (ebook) |
    DDC 346.7302/9--dc23
LC record available at https://lccn.loc.gov/2016031685

This book covers only United States law, unless it specifically states otherwise.

Please note

We believe accurate, plain-English legal information should help you solve many of
your own legal problems. But this text is not a substitute for personalized advice from
a knowledgeable lawyer. If you want the help of a trained professional—and we'll
always point out situations in which we think that's a good idea—consult an attorney
licensed to practice in your state.

Acknowledgments

I've been privileged to work with the talented editorial and production teams at Nolo for more than two decades. First, I'd like to thank Mary Randolph, Denis Clifford, and Barbara Kate Repa for generously sharing their time, ideas, and earlier work on health care directives and financial powers of attorney. This book stands on a strong foundation they helped me to build. Thanks, too, to Mary for her always insightful editing on earlier editions of this book.

In addition, I'd like to thank Jaleh Doane, for carefully shepherding every edition of this book and all of the forms through production—from design and layout to final printing. For this edition, my gratitude also goes to Susan Putney for her careful production work.

Last but in no means least, a million thanks to my husband, Stewart, for his encouragement and support.

About the Author

Shae Irving has been part of Nolo's editorial team since 1994, specializing in estate planning issues. She has written or cowritten books and software, including *Prenuptial Agreements: How to Write a Fair & Lasting Contract*, *Get It Together: Organize Your Records So Your Family Won't Have To*, and Nolo's *Quicken WillMaker Plus* software. Irving graduated from Berkeley Law at the University of California.

Table of Contents

Your Living Will and Power of Attorney Companion 1

1 Planning Ahead—An Overview 3

Why You Should Plan for Incapacity 4

Using Medical Directives 7

Using a Durable Power of Attorney for Finances 10

The Mental Capacity Requirement 11

Will You Need a Lawyer? 12

If a Loved One Needs Help 12

Other Important Issues to Consider 13

2 Advance Health Care Directives 17

How Advance Directives Work 18

About Your Health Care Agent 22

Preparing Your Advance Directive 26

What to Do After You Complete Your Advance Directive 46

Revoking an Advance Directive 48

3 Do Not Resuscitate (DNR) and POLST Forms 51

How DNR Forms Work 52

Preparing a DNR Form 52

What to Do After You Complete a DNR Form 54

Revoking a DNR Form 54

About POLST Forms 54

4 Durable Powers of Attorney for Finances 59

How Durable Powers of Attorney for Finances Work 60

About Your Agent for Finances 70

Preparing Your Durable Power of Attorney 79

Making Your Durable Power of Attorney Legal 96

Revoking a Durable Power of Attorney for Finances 101

5 Help Beyond the Book 107

Legal Document Assistants 108

Lawyers 108

Getting More Information on Your Own 109

Appendixes

A **How to Use the Interactive Forms on Nolo.com** 111

Editing RTFs: General Instructions 112

Downloadable Files 113

B **Forms** 115

Index 141

Your Living Will and Power of Attorney Companion

As we all know, unexpected accidents and illnesses happen every day. Without warning, family members are often asked to make medical decisions and take care of financial matters for a loved one who becomes injured or ill. With only a few simple legal forms, you can put important medical and financial decisions in the hands of those you trust—and give them invaluable guidance for making what can be difficult decisions.

The forms in this book let you do three essential things:

- state the kinds of medical treatment you do or do not want
- name someone to carry out those health care wishes and make other necessary medical decisions for you, and
- name someone to handle financial matters for you if you can no longer manage them on your own.

You can accomplish these tasks by completing two or three of the following basic legal forms, each of which is offered and explained in this book:

Advance Health Care Directive. Also called a "living will," this is the official California form that lets you state your wishes for health care and name a trusted person who will work with doctors and other health care providers to be sure you get the kind of care you want. You can also use your advance health care directive to name the doctor you'd like to supervise your care, express your wishes about organ donation, and note what kind of body disposition and other final arrangements you would like. (A downloadable bonus guide provides more guidance on making final arrangements in advance.)

Do Not Resuscitate (DNR) Form. Some people who don't want to receive life-prolonging treatment when close to death may also want to prepare a DNR form. If a medical emergency occurs, this form alerts emergency medical personnel that you do not wish to receive cardiopulmonary resuscitation (CPR).

A close cousin to the DNR form is a California document known as a POLST. POLST stands for "Physician Orders for Life-Sustaining Treatment," and it's a form that can dictate not only your resuscitation preferences but other end-of-life care wishes as well. A POLST form is used only in a hospital or other medical care setting, and a health care provider can help you make one.

Durable Power of Attorney for Finances. This official California form allows you to appoint the person of your choice to manage your finances for you if someday you can no longer do so yourself. If you prepare this document, you won't have to worry about who will pay your bills, manage your investments, handle your insurance claims, or take care of other essential financial tasks.

The forms in this book are straightforward and easy to complete—either by hand or using your computer. (You'll find them as tear-outs at the back of the book, or you can download them for free from Nolo's website, using the link below.) We give you detailed instructions and suggestions so that your documents will reflect your wishes. You probably won't need a lawyer's help, but we'll alert you to the few situations where legal advice might be helpful or necessary.

Everyone should do at least a little bit of planning—it's a great gift to your family. And with these simple forms, you can have a sound plan in place in a matter of hours.

Get Forms, Updates, and More at This Book's Companion Page on Nolo.com

You can download the forms and worksheets in this book at

www.nolo.com/back-of-book/CPOA.html

When there are important changes to the information in this book, we'll post updates on the same page. You'll find other useful information on this book's companion page, too, such as a free guide to making final arrangements and a podcast from the author. (See Appendix A for a list of forms and resources available at Nolo.com.)

Planning Ahead—An Overview

Why You Should Plan for Incapacity 4

    Getting the Care You Want 4

    Helping Those Who Care About You 6

    Avoiding Conservatorship Proceedings 6

Using Medical Directives 7

    Advance Health Care Directive 7

    Do Not Resuscitate (DNR) Form 8

Using a Durable Power of Attorney for Finances 10

    Do You Need a Durable Power of Attorney? 10

    When You Shouldn't Rely on a Durable Power of Attorney 11

The Mental Capacity Requirement 11

Will You Need a Lawyer? 12

If a Loved One Needs Help 12

Other Important Issues to Consider 13

    Long-Term Care 13

    Arranging Care for Young Children 14

    Leaving Your Property 15

    Winding Up Your Affairs After Death 15

If you're like most people, you aren't eager to spend time thinking about what would happen if you became unable to take care of yourself because of illness, an accident, or advanced age. It can be just as difficult to contemplate what would happen if a loved one, perhaps an aging parent or an ailing partner, reaches that stage. But sometimes it's impossible to avoid these issues. You may find yourself wondering: Who would pay my bills and take care of my house if I got sick? How would doctors know what kind of medical care I want to receive if I were hurt in an accident and couldn't tell them myself? Who's going to take care of Mom's finances when her Alzheimer's disease grows worse?

If you don't do at least a little bit of planning—naming a trusted person to direct medical care and handle finances—these personal matters could wind up in the hands of doctors or in front of courts who may know very little about what you would prefer. It's far better to spend a few hours completing the legal documents that will make your wishes clear.

As you think about your preferences for health care and property management, you may be surprised by the range of concerns that arise. In addition to practical and financial considerations, there will surely be emotional aspects to the choices you make. Your own feelings, values, and personal relationships will shape many of your decisions. For many people, making end-of-life medical decisions will also be a time for spiritual reflection and inquiry.

While this book can't address all of the practical, emotional, and spiritual elements of planning for a time when you may need help with basic care, it can help you understand your options and ensure that there won't be legal complications down the road.

This chapter introduces the subject of incapacity and how to plan ahead for the time when help may be necessary. It explains the process and briefly describes the legal forms you will need. Chapters 2, 3, and 4 show you how to complete your forms.

The California Probate Code

Throughout this book you will see many citations to the California Probate Code. These citations look something like this: Cal. Prob. Code § 4000. The California Probate Code is the body of laws that governs the forms contained in this book—and most other things having to do with planning for incapacity and estate planning in California. The last number in the citation is important—it's the section of the code where you can find the actual law (also called a statute) supporting what we say. If you ever want to read the law itself, all you have to do is go online or visit a law library to look up the section number. Chapter 5 explains how.

You can also use this book if you are helping someone else to plan ahead and make the necessary documents. (See "If a Loved One Needs Help," later in this chapter, for a discussion of some of the unique issues you may face.)

Why You Should Plan for Incapacity

Almost every adult can benefit from some planning for incapacity. Below are a few important reasons to take the time to make at least the basic documents directing your medical care and financial management—as well as to consider some of the other planning methods discussed at the end of this chapter.

Getting the Care You Want

Making an advance directive for health care and a power of attorney for finances is the best way—and sometimes the only way—to ensure that you will get the kind of care you want. If you don't make documents directing your health care, you might receive treatment that is very different from what you would have wished. And if you don't authorize someone to oversee your finances, a court could put those matters into the hands of someone you'd never choose for the job.

"Living Will" or "Advance Directive"?

You've probably heard the term "living will." That's the name commonly given to the document in which you state your preferences for health care if you are someday unable to communicate those wishes. People are usually most concerned with stating their wishes about the use of medical technology at the very end of life.

In California, a living will goes by a different name: advance health care directive. This document lets you do more than you can do in a traditional living will. You can use it to state your health care wishes in detail and to take care of other important tasks discussed later in this chapter.

This book uses the term advance health care directive, not living will. But you can rest assured that the document it offers is the one you need to ensure that your wishes are clearly communicated and carefully followed.

It's especially important to plan ahead if you think it's likely that family members won't understand your wishes, or if a court might appoint someone other than your first choice to make decisions for you. For example, planning is essential if you are a member of an unmarried couple, straight or same-sex, and you want your partner to take responsibility for your health care and finances if someday you need help. Without the right legal documents, a court could choose another family member to make financial decisions on your behalf.

Benefits for Domestic Partners in California

Though same-sex marriage has been legal in California for several years, many couples still have valid domestic partnerships, and it is still possible to register a new domestic partnership with the state.

In California, registered domestic partners have as much authority to make medical decisions for each other as spouses do. (Cal. Prob. Code § 4716.) And if a court must appoint someone to make medical or financial decisions on your behalf, your registered domestic partner (or someone nominated by your partner) gets the highest preference—again, the same as a spouse. (Cal. Prob. Code § 1812.)

The law requires you to register your partnership with the state to qualify for these benefits. You and your partner may register if:

- you live together
- you agree to be responsible for each other's basic living expenses for as long as your partnership lasts
- neither of you is married or the member of another currently registered domestic partnership
- you are not related by blood in a way that would prevent you from being married in California
- you are each at least 18 years old, and
- you are both capable of consenting to the domestic partnership.

In addition, you must meet one of the following requirements:

- you are of the same sex, or
- one or both of you is over the age of 62 and one or both of you meets the eligibility criteria for insurance benefits under Title II of the Social Security Act (42 U.S.C. § 402(a)) or the eligibility requirements for benefits under Title XVI of the Social Security Act (42 U.S.C. § 1381).

For information about domestic partnership registration and the forms you need to register, visit the Secretary of State's website at www.sos.ca.gov/registries/domestic-partners-registry or call the office at 916-653-3984.

It's also crucial to make a plan if you feel strongly about any of the details of your medical care or financial management. Only you know the particulars of your wishes—for example, that you never want to be placed on a respirator or that your house shouldn't be sold while you are alive, even if you can no longer live there. Writing down these finer points is the best way to prevent them from being lost.

Helping Those Who Care About You

Writing down your wishes now can be a great help to those close to you if you ever become unable to care for yourself. In fact, your family members and close friends are likely to look upon your planning as a minor miracle. It means that loved ones won't have to spend long, agonizing hours (and sometimes a lot of money) trying to sort out what you would want, perhaps facing disagreements and disputes among themselves as they do so. Even well-meaning family members can and do argue about decisions relating to health care and money. Especially during a stressful time, different people may sincerely and strongly disagree about what's best for you.

By stating your wishes in advance, you may not take care of any discomfort others might have about your preferences—but most people will respect what you have asked for and accept your plan. And anyone who wants to challenge your documents will probably be unsuccessful, facing a losing battle in court unless he or she can show that you were not of sound mind when you made your plan, or that you signed documents under duress or as the result of fraud.

Avoiding Conservatorship Proceedings

It may be easiest to understand why it's so important to plan ahead by considering in more detail what can happen if you don't.

If you have not made documents directing your health care and you become incapacitated, the doctors who take care of you will suggest what kind of medical care you should receive and turn to family members for decisions. Problems often arise when family members disagree among themselves—or when family members and partners disagree—about what treatment is proper. The most common result is that emotions run high as family members and loved ones take sides in an attempt to take care of you in the way they think best, with all involved sincerely believing they have your best interest at heart.

In the most complicated scenarios, these battles over medical care wind up in court. If that happens, a judge, who usually has little medical knowledge and no familiarity with you, is called upon to decide the future of your treatment, usually by giving one person power to make health care decisions for you. (This person is called a "conservator.") Such battles are costly, time consuming, and painful to those involved—and they are unnecessary if you have the foresight to use a formal document to express your wishes for your health care.

If you don't make a document naming someone to manage your finances, similar battles may ensue. Without the necessary document, your relatives or other loved ones will have to ask a judge to name a conservator to manage your finances.

The upshot of all this is that, without a couple of simple legal documents prepared in advance, a court may have to appoint a conservator to take care of your medical care, your finances, or both. Conservatorship proceedings can be complicated, expensive, and embarrassing. Your loved ones must ask the court to rule that you cannot take care of yourself—a public airing of a very private matter. Court proceedings are matters of public record; in some places, a notice may even be published in a local newspaper. If relatives fight over who is to be the conservator, the proceedings will surely become even more disagreeable, sometimes downright nasty. And all of this causes costs to mount up, especially if lawyers must be hired.

What's more, if a conservator is appointed to handle your finances, conservatorship proceedings are just the beginning of court involvement. Often a conservator of property must:

- post a bond—a kind of insurance policy that pays if the conservator steals or misuses property
- prepare (or hire a lawyer to prepare) detailed reports and periodically file them with the court, and
- get court approval for certain transactions, such as selling real estate or making slightly risky investments.

Conservators in charge of your personal care—including health care decisions—may be required to report to a court as well.

You can see why it's usually far less burdensome to take the time to prepare an advance directive and a power of attorney. There are only a very few situations in which a conservatorship might actually be desirable; these are discussed in upcoming sections of this chapter.

Using Medical Directives

Let's take a brief look at the two health care documents you can make with this book.

Advance Health Care Directive

In California, the document you use to direct your health care is called an advance health care directive. California's advance directive form permits you to do several important things. Each of the topics introduced here is covered in detail in Chapter 2.

Name someone to carry out your health care wishes and make other medical decisions for you. The first part of the advance directive form is called a "durable power of attorney for health care." A power of attorney is simply a legal document that you use to name someone to make decisions for you or take action on your behalf. The word "attorney" here means anyone authorized to act for you; that person definitely doesn't have to be a lawyer.

A power of attorney is considered "durable" if it stays in effect even after you are incapacitated. Powers of attorney that aren't durable are not valid if you are no longer able to make your own decisions.

You use this part of the form, the durable power of attorney, to name the person who will make sure your health care preferences are honored and who will make any other necessary medical decisions for you. This person is called your "health care agent," or simply your "agent." Most people name their spouse, partner, or a grown child as agent. It's best to appoint just one agent and name a backup in case that person is unable to serve. The form allows you to name up to two alternate agents.

The advance directive gives your agent broad authority to make health care decisions on your behalf, though if you choose, you can limit your agent's authority when you complete your document.

When You Might Not Want to Appoint an Agent for Health Care

It's never a bad idea to write out your health care wishes. Doing so can only help you get the kind of treatment you want. There is one circumstance, however, in which it may not be wise to appoint a health care agent. You shouldn't do it if you don't know anyone that you trust with the job. Your agent functions without court supervision (that's the point of naming one), so it's critical that you choose someone who can understand your wishes and is willing and able to be your advocate if necessary. (More on this in Chapter 2.)

If you don't know anyone who fits this bill, it's usually better to let a court appoint a conservator for you, if necessary. A conservator must report to a judge, who can be certain that the conservator is acting in your best interests.

Advance Directives and California's New Aid-in-Dying Law: What You Need to Know

In 2016, California passed a law allowing certain terminally ill patients to request a prescription for life-ending medication. (This is sometimes known as "death with dignity," or "physician-assisted suicide," though "aid-in-dying" is the correct legal term.) To request such a prescription in California, a patient must be:

- at least 18 years old
- a California resident
- mentally capable of making and communicating health care decisions, and
- diagnosed with a terminal disease that will result in death within six months.

In addition, the patient must meet many strict procedural requirements to use the new law.

Aid-in-dying cannot be requested with an advance directive because, when an advance directive takes effect, the patient typically lacks the required mental capacity to request the prescription. Nor is it legally possible to give a health care agent the power to request such a prescription on your behalf. California continues to be explicit that aid-in-dying is outside the scope of its advance directive laws. (Cal. Prob. Code § 4653.)

To find out more about aid-in-dying, discuss your concerns with a supportive health care provider. Because the law is new, the person you ask may be getting educated, too—but a responsible provider should be able to point you toward good, local resources for learning more.

State your health care wishes. You can state your preferences for medical treatment in as little or as much detail as you like. For example, you can indicate whether or not you want to receive life-prolonging treatment—a respirator, CPR, surgery, and the like—if you are close to death from a terminal illness, in a permanent coma, or if your agent (after consulting with your doctor) determines that treatment would be more likely to put you at risk than to help you. You can choose from general statements about your wishes, or you can write out as many specifics as you like about the kinds of treatments you do or do not wish to receive under various circumstances. We guide you through your options, providing samples you can use if you want to include detailed wishes in your form.

Specify whether you wish to donate organs, tissues, or body parts after your death. If you want to donate any of your organs or body parts after death, the advance directive form contains a place for you to say so.

Name the primary physician who will be responsible for your care. If you have an established relationship with a doctor whom you trust, you may want to specify that this doctor supervise your care, working with your health care agent.

Unless you indicate otherwise, your advance directive becomes effective only if your doctor determines that you are incapacitated and unable to communicate your wishes for care. If you prefer, however, you can allow your health care agent—not a doctor—to decide when to put your document into effect.

PODCAST
Learn by listening. Visit Nolo's website to hear a podcast on the subject of living wills and medical directives. See Appendix A for the link.

Do Not Resuscitate (DNR) Form

If, in your advance directive, you state that you do not wish to receive life-sustaining treatment, you may also want to consider preparing a simple form called a Prehospital Do Not Resuscitate (DNR) Form. (In California, this is sometimes known as a "Request to Forgo Resuscitative Measures," but we call it by its less cumbersome and more common name.)

The Five Wishes Document: Should You Use It?

You may have heard of "Five Wishes," an easy-to-prepare advance directive said to be legally valid in almost every state, including California. While it is true that Five Wishes complies with the letter of the law in California, we don't recommend that you use it as your official advance directive.

The laws governing advance directives include plenty of state-specific provisions, such as terms, definitions, and procedures that California health care providers know and trust. The generic language of Five Wishes could create confusion, delays, or—at worst—legal tussles, which is exactly what advance directives seek to avoid.

That said, the Five Wishes form can help you think through the issues involved in end-of-life care—and that can make it easier to discuss these matters with your loved ones. You can view a free copy of the document or download a printable copy for a few dollars at the Aging with Dignity website: www.agingwithdignity.org.

A prehospital DNR form is used for the specific and limited purpose of alerting emergency medical personnel to the fact that you do not wish to receive cardiopulmonary resuscitation (CPR) in the event of a medical emergency. This means that if you are anywhere other than in the hospital—for example, at home, in a long-term care facility, or outside somewhere—and you collapse, the paramedics who respond to the emergency will not attempt to restart your heart or your breathing. (Hospital emergency rooms are also strongly encouraged to honor prehospital DNR forms, and most will do so.) If you are already in the hospital, you can ask your doctor to place a DNR order in your medical record; there's no need to create a separate form.

DNR forms or orders are sometimes used by those who:

- have a terminal illness

- are at increased risk for cardiac or respiratory arrest, or
- oppose the use of CPR under any circumstances.

If you know you don't want to receive CPR in an emergency, preparing a DNR form is a good idea. If you don't have one, emergency medical personnel will do all they can to save your life, including administering CPR. Even if you've prepared an advance directive stating that you don't wish to receive CPR, emergency teams won't likely know of its existence.

DNR Form v. DNR Order: Is There a Difference?

As described just above, when you are not in the hospital, the DNR document you'll make is officially called a "Prehospital Do Not Resuscitate (DNR) Form." Once you're admitted to a hospital, the instructions placed in your medical record are known as a "DNR order." In either case, a doctor must sign off on your wishes to make them legally valid. Perhaps most important, a DNR form and a DNR order have the same function and, as a practical matter, the two terms are often used interchangeably.

In addition to preparing the DNR form, you will want to get a MedicAlert bracelet or medallion to wear so that your wishes will be obvious to medical personnel. We explain how to complete the form and obtain a medallion in Chapter 3.

What's a POLST Form?

A POLST form—short for Physician Orders for Life-Sustaining Treatment—is similar to a DNR order and may also contain other critical care wishes, but is not a substitute for an advance directive. In Chapter 3, we explain how POLST forms may sometimes be used instead of, or in addition to, DNR orders.

Using a Durable Power of Attorney for Finances

A durable power of attorney for finances (DPAF) allows you to name someone to take care of your financial matters if you become incapacitated and can't handle them yourself. ("Durable" simply means that the document stays in effect after you are incapacitated.) You can make the document effective immediately, if you need or want help right away. Or you can make what's known as a "springing" durable power of attorney—a document that doesn't take effect unless and until you become incapacitated.

The trusted person you name—again, called your "agent"—will have whatever financial powers you grant to him or her. You can authorize your agent to pay bills (with your assets), make bank deposits, claim government benefits, manage your investments, and handle many other financial matters.

As you begin thinking about appointing an agent, keep in mind that it's usually best to name just one person, and that it's wise for this to be the same person you named to make health care decisions for you. If that's not possible, it's critical that you name two people who can work well together.

Most people with property or an income can benefit from making a durable power of attorney for finances. (We show you how in Chapter 4.) But it's not the right document in every situation. Following are some answers to common questions about when you should—and shouldn't—rely on a durable power of attorney for finances.

Do You Need a Durable Power of Attorney?

You may not think that you need a durable power of attorney for finances if you're married, or if you've put most of your property into a living trust or hold it in joint tenancy. But the truth is that in all of these situations, a durable power of attorney can make life much easier for your family if you become incapacitated.

If you are married or have a registered domestic partner. Don't assume that your spouse or domestic partner will automatically be able to manage your finances if you can't. Your spouse or partner does have some authority over property you own together—for example, to pay bills from a joint bank account or sell stock in a joint brokerage account. There are significant limits, however, on your spouse's or partner's right to sell property owned by both of you. For example, both of you must agree to the sale of co-owned real estate or cars. Because an incapacitated spouse or partner can't consent to such a sale, the other's hands are tied.

And when it comes to property that belongs only to you, your spouse or partner has no legal authority. You must use a durable power of attorney to give your spouse or partner authority over your property.

If you have a living trust. If you've made a revocable living trust, you know that its primary purpose is to avoid probate. But the trust can also be useful if you become incapable of taking care of your financial affairs. That's because the person who will distribute trust property after your death (called the successor trustee) can also, in most cases, take over management of the trust property if you become incapacitated. Usually, the trust document gives the successor trustee authority to manage all property in the trust and to use it for your needs.

However, the successor trustee has no authority over property not held in trust. Most people transfer into a living trust assets that are expensive to probate, such as real estate and valuable securities, but few people hold all their property in a living trust. So although it's helpful, a living trust isn't a complete substitute for a durable power of attorney for finances.

If you own joint tenancy property. Joint tenancy is a way for two or more poeple to own property together. The most notable feature of joint tenancy is that when one owner dies, the other owners automatically inherit the deceased person's share of the property. But if you become incapacitated, the other owners have very limited authority over your share of the joint tenancy property. For example, if you and someone else own a bank account in joint tenancy and one of you becomes incapacitated, the other owner is legally entitled to use the funds. The healthy joint tenant can take care of the financial needs of the incapacitated person simply by paying bills from the joint account. But the other account owner has no legal right to endorse checks made out to the incapacitated person. In practice, it might be possible—if not technically legal—to get an incapacitated person's checks into a joint account by stamping them "For Deposit Only," but that's not the easiest way to handle things.

Matters get even more complicated with other kinds of joint tenancy property. Real estate is a good example. If one owner becomes incapacitated, the other has no legal authority to sell or refinance the incapacitated owner's share.

By contrast, with a durable power of attorney, you can give your agent authority over your share of joint tenancy property, including real estate and bank accounts.

When You Shouldn't Rely on a Durable Power of Attorney

As discussed earlier, the expense and intrusion of a conservatorship are rarely desirable. In a few situations, however, special concerns make a conservatorship preferable to giving someone authority under a durable power of attorney.

You want court supervision of your finances. If you can't think of someone you trust enough to appoint as your agent, with broad authority over your property and finances, don't create

a durable power of attorney for finances. A conservatorship, with the built-in safeguard of court supervision, is worth the extra cost and trouble.

You fear family fights. A durable power of attorney is a readily accepted and powerful legal document. Once you've finalized yours, anyone who wants to challenge your plans for financial management will face a tough, and probably losing, battle in court. But if you expect that family members will challenge your document or make continual trouble for your agent, a conservatorship may be preferable. Your relatives may still fight, but at least the court will be there to keep an eye on your welfare and your property.

SEE AN EXPERT

If you're undecided. If you expect family fights and feel uncomfortable making a durable power of attorney for finances, you may want to talk with a knowledgeable lawyer. An expert can help you weigh your concerns and options, and help you decide whether a durable power of attorney is the best choice for you.

The Mental Capacity Requirement

To make a health care directive or power of attorney for finances, you must be of sound mind. In other words, you cannot make valid documents if you are already incapacitated.

In terms of your medical care, you are of sound mind as long as you can understand the nature and consequences of your health care choices (including significant benefits, risks, and alternatives) and communicate your wishes for care.

For money matters, your mental capacity is determined by a similar standard. You are mentally competent as long as you can understand the rights, responsibilities, risks, or benefits involved in your financial decisions, and the potential consequences of what you decide.

If you have physical disabilities but are otherwise able to understand your health care and financial choices, your documents will be perfectly valid.

When you sign a document, no one makes a determination about your mental state. The issue will come up later only if someone goes to court and challenges the document, claiming that you weren't of sound mind when you signed it. That kind of lawsuit is very rare.

Even in the highly unlikely event of a court hearing, the competency requirement is not difficult to satisfy. If you understood what you were doing when you signed your medical directive or power of attorney, that's enough. To make this determination, a judge would probably question those who knew you well at the time you made your document. There would be no general inquiry into your life. It wouldn't matter, for example, that you were occasionally forgetful or absentminded around the time when you signed your power of attorney document or health care directive.

> **SEE AN EXPERT**
>
> **Heading off problems.** If you think someone is likely to go to court and challenge your documents or claim that you were coerced into signing them, see a good estate planning lawyer. The lawyer can review the documents you create yourself or draw up documents for you. (This is not necessary in most circumstances, as discussed next.) An experienced lawyer can also answer any questions you have about your documents directing medical care and financial management—and about other estate planning documents. For example, you may also be expecting challenges to your will or a trust. You can talk with a lawyer about all of these issues. Your attorney can also testify about your mental competency, should the need arise.

Will You Need a Lawyer?

You can probably prepare the documents in this book without any help from a lawyer. In fact, the California advance directive and power of attorney forms are designed so that people can complete them easily, without professional assistance.

If, however, you have specific questions or unusual circumstances—for example, unusually contentious family members or a very large amount of property—you may need legal advice. As you read this book, you'll be alerted to circumstances where you may run into trouble and benefit from a lawyer's help. If you do need to see a lawyer, the information in Chapter 5 can help you find a good one.

If a Loved One Needs Help

Many people find themselves in the painful position of seeing a family member or close friend lose the ability to make sound medical and financial decisions. In addition to the grief of watching a loved one's condition deteriorate, a caretaker's situation can be made more difficult if the person in need of help denies—or is oblivious to—worsening physical or mental health.

If the person you're caring for is of sound mind (see above) and receptive to the idea of setting out medical wishes and naming someone to watch over medical and financial decisions, that makes things much easier. You can use this book to explain the process, answer questions, and help prepare and finalize the right documents. But if you think someone who needs help will resist your efforts, you need to carefully consider the way you approach the subject.

For some stubborn folks, it may be enough to explain why planning is important. Some people may be moved by a request to plan ahead because it will relieve much anxiety and pressure for you and the others who care about them, even if they don't much care what happens or who makes decisions for them. Others may be more inclined to make health care and financial documents if they understand that doing so is the best way for them to stay in control of their lives, because whomever they name must follow their instructions in every way possible. Of course, when you talk with anyone who's struggling with increasing frailty, you will have to tread very gently around issues of deteriorating mental or physical abilities, perhaps underscoring that planning is a good thing for *anybody* to do, just in case it's necessary someday.

All that said, it's just as important to remember that legally you can't—and you shouldn't—try to force someone to follow a certain course just because you think it's best. If you strong-arm or coerce someone into making documents and those documents are later challenged in court, you could find yourself in serious legal trouble. The same goes for faking signatures on any legal documents. Don't do it. If your loved one doesn't want to cooperate and you eventually have to ask a court for control over his or her affairs, that may be difficult, but it's much better than being charged with fraud or forgery. Under California law, you could be forced to pay at least $10,000 if a court finds you guilty of such behavior. (Cal. Prob. Code § 4742(b).)

RESOURCE

If it's too late to plan. If a family member is already incapacitated and you need to ask a court to name a conservator, you can learn more by visiting the California Courts Self-Help Center at www.courts. ca.gov/selfhelp-conservatorship.htm.

RESOURCE

Getting support. The following resources may help you cope with some of the stresses of caregiving.

The 36-Hour Day, by Nancy L. Mace and Peter V. Rabins (The Johns Hopkins University Press), is a comprehensive guide to caring for people with Alzheimer's disease, as well as other types of dementia and memory loss.

The Family Caregiver Alliance is a support organization and information clearinghouse for families and friends providing care for someone who is incapacitated. You can browse their offerings at www. caregiver.org.

The National Alzheimer's Association provides resources and support for people caring for a loved one with Alzheimer's disease. You can find lots of free information on the organization's website at www.alz. org. You can also contact them by mail or phone: 225 North Michigan Avenue, Floor 17, Chicago, IL 60601-7633, 800-272-3900.

Other Important Issues to Consider

Making the most important documents in this book—the advance health care directive and the durable power of attorney for finances—will take you a long way in your planning. Once you've completed them, you can be confident that someone you trust will be on hand to take care of you, personally and financially. But there are a few other things you should consider when thinking ahead. Here is a brief look at the most important of them.

Long-Term Care

Someday, you or a close family member may need some kind of long-term care. A significant number of older people, even if they remain basically healthy, develop physical or mental frailties or impairments that at some point prevent them from living independent lives.

"Long-term care" may be defined in many ways, but essentially it means regular assistance with medical care or personal needs—for example, eating, dressing, bathing, or moving around—provided by someone other than a family member. There are many types of long-term care available these days, ranging from part-time home care, to adult day care, to independent living and assisted living residential communities, to nursing facilities. Some long-term care is temporary—for example, if you're recovering from a broken hip or a stroke. In other cases, permanent care is necessary.

The need for temporary or permanent care raises a number of difficult questions:

- What kind of care is needed?
- Who will provide it?
- Where will it be provided?
- How much will it cost?
- Who will pay for it?

If you appoint an agent for health care and finances and you do nothing else, you won't be left out in the cold when it comes to long-term care. Your agent will most likely be the one to find answers to these questions and try to get you the care you need. You can make the job much easier by thinking about, talking about, and planning for potential needs ahead of time. Discussing your preferences and making a plan for financing necessary care—including an evaluation of long-term care insurance and potentially available government benefits—will save your agent and other family members a lot of time, trouble, and money down the road.

 RESOURCE

Help with long-term care decisions. *Long-Term Care: How to Plan & Pay for It*, by Joseph L. Matthews (Nolo), can help you understand the many alternatives to nursing facilities and show you how to fit the care you need to the funds you have available. Topics covered include arranging in-home care, finding a non-nursing facility residence, choosing a nursing home, getting the most out of Medicare and other benefit programs, evaluating long-term care insurance, protecting your assets when the costs of care start to mount, and other important matters.

Who Decides Where You Will Live?

If you become incapacitated and are unable to continue living at home, you may wonder who will make the decision about where you will live. California law permits you to use your durable power of attorney for health care to give your health care agent the authority to decide where you will reside. (Cal. Prob. Code § 4671.) However, you should remember that it's your agent for *finances* who will have the authority to pay for the costs of your living arrangements. This brings up an important point, discussed in both Chapters 2 and 4: It's almost always best to name the same person as your agent for health care and finances. If you can't name just one person for some reason, it's critical that you name two people who can work well together and make decisions as a team.

In any case, it's a very good idea to spend some time thinking about where you would want to live if you could no longer live at home. If you want to remain at home or with relatives as long as possible, taking advantage of the benefits of in-home care—or if you have a care facility in mind—you should speak to your health care agent, agent for finances, and close family and friends about your wishes. This will help them make the best decision for you. You may even want to note these wishes in your advance health care directive. If your agents or family members ever have a bad squabble over your living arrangements and wind up in court (not likely, but it has happened), your notes will help the judge understand your preferences.

Arranging Care for Young Children

You can't use a power of attorney to give anyone authority to care for your minor children (those under 18) if you become incapacitated. In your durable power of attorney for finances, you can give your agent the authority to pay for the children's needs out of your assets—but the agent's power under the document stops there. If you become incapacitated, your children's other parent will be responsible for taking care of them. If the other parent is not available, a court will appoint someone—a close family member, if possible—to do it.

In California, if you have been diagnosed with a terminal illness, you may ask a court to nominate another person as a "joint guardian" along with you. (Cal. Prob. Code § 2105(f).) This process is intended to alleviate some of the emotional stress and disruption kids suffer when a parent becomes seriously ill and later dies. The joint guardian has the same rights and responsibilities for your child as you do. The court can't appoint a joint guardian over the objection of your child's other parent unless it first finds that granting custody to the other parent would be bad for the child.

Under circumstances other than terminal illness, to name a guardian who will care for your young children if you die, you should write a will (see below). The court will give strong weight to your recommendation when appointing the guardian. (There is no need to name a guardian in your will if a court appoints a joint guardian when you are terminally ill. The person appointed by the court will continue to care for your children after you die.)

Leaving Your Property

If you're thinking about end-of-life issues, you'll probably want to make some decisions about who will receive your property when you die. You can use a will, a living trust, or another legal transfer method (such as joint tenancy ownership) to carry out your wishes. Along with deciding how property will be distributed, you may want to explore strategies for avoiding probate—the time-consuming and often wasteful court proceedings after death. And if you're very wealthy, you will probably want to explore methods of eliminating or reducing estate taxes.

The easiest thing to do is to draw up a simple will. This is important if you own any property that matters to you, so that it will be passed on as you wish. And, as mentioned above, it's critical if you have kids under 18. People with young children should write a will to nominate a guardian who will raise their children if they can't, and they should make a plan for how the children's property will be managed. (Minors, by law, can't control any significant amount of property they own.)

Below, you'll find a list of resources from Nolo that can help you with wills, trusts, and other estate planning matters.

Winding Up Your Affairs After Death

With one important exception, you can't give an agent the power to handle tasks after your death, such as paying your debts or transferring property to the people who inherit it. The exception is this: Your agent for health care is permitted to handle the disposition of your body after your death, including donating organs, authorizing an autopsy, and handling funeral arrangements, unless you say otherwise in your advance health care directive.

If you want an agent to have authority to wind up the rest of your affairs after death, use your will to name that person as your executor. If you also plan to avoid probate, you may want to prepare a living trust and name that person as your successor trustee—the person who will manage and distribute trust property after your death.

RESOURCE

More information from Nolo about estate planning. You may want to start at www.nolo.com, where you'll find lots of helpful information about estate planning. You can read free articles on a wide variety of estate planning topics and—when you're ready—you can make estate planning documents online, including a will and living trust.

Here are some of the other estate planning resources offered by Nolo:

Quicken WillMaker Plus (software for Windows) allows you to prepare a comprehensive will using your computer. It also enables you to prepare a final arrangements document and many other useful legal forms.

Plan Your Estate, by Denis Clifford, offers in-depth coverage of all significant elements of estate planning, from simple wills to probate avoidance and complex tax-saving trusts.

Quick & Legal Will Book, by Denis Clifford, shows you how to prepare a will that covers your needs, including basic trusts for minor children.

Make Your Own Living Trust, by Denis Clifford, provides a complete explanation of how to prepare a probate avoidance living trust, including the forms you'll need.

8 Ways to Avoid Probate, by Mary Randolph, offers a thorough discussion of all the major ways to avoid probate by transferring property at death outside of a will.

The Executor's Guide: Settling a Loved One's Estate or Trust, by Mary Randolph, provides a detailed explanation of an executor's duties and details about how to wrap up an estate.

Making Final Arrangements

Do your family members know what kind of body disposition and memorial ceremonies you want after your death? If they don't, it may be very difficult for them to make these decisions at a time when they are already feeling overwhelmed. Planning in this area can also help save some money; funeral and related costs can be very expensive.

Your advance health care directive is a fine place to make some notes about the final arrangements that you want. If you have the time and the inclination, you can write a statement or a letter setting out your wishes and attach it to your advance directive. This way, your survivors will have your wishes at hand when the time comes.

FORM

Help with final arrangements. When it comes to making final arrangements in advance, there's much to consider: Will your body be buried or cremated? What kind of funeral or memorial service would you like? Do you want to decide about details such as a casket, burial marker, or epitaph? And what about setting aside funds to cover the costs? Most people benefit from some assistance with their plans. Start by checking out the free, downloadable guide, "Making Final Arrangements," on the Nolo website (see Appendix A for the link).

Advance Health Care Directives

How Advance Directives Work..18

    Who Can Make an Advance Directive..18

    When Your Advance Directive Takes Effect 18

    Duty of Medical Personnel to Honor Your Advance Directive...19

    When Your Advance Directive Ends...20

About Your Health Care Agent 22

    Your Agent's Powers 23

    What Your Health Care Agent Can't Do..24

    Your Health Care Agent's Legal Responsibilities..24

    Choosing Your Health Care Agent..24

    If You Do Not Name a Health Care Agent 26

Preparing Your Advance Directive..26

    Part 1: Power of Attorney for Health Care..26

    Part 2: Instructions for Health Care...29

    Part 3: Donation of Organs at Death...36

    Part 4: Primary Physician 37

    Part 5: Making Your Advance Directive Legal...38

What to Do After You Complete Your Advance Directive..46

    Distributing Copies...46

    Talking With Doctors..47

    Talking With Family Members and Friends..47

    Preparing a Wallet Card 47

    Keeping Your Documents Up to Date..48

Revoking an Advance Directive...48

To ensure that your preferences for medical care will be understood and followed, you will want to prepare an Advance Health Care Directive. As described in Chapter 1, with a California advance directive you can:

- write out specific instructions that describe the medical care you do or do not want if you can no longer express your wishes, and
- name someone you trust to supervise your wishes and direct your health care in any situations that you don't cover in your written instructions.

If you like, you can also use your advance directive to name the primary physician you want to be responsible for your care, and you can state whether you wish to donate any organs or body parts after your death.

How Advance Directives Work

You have a constitutional right to control your own medical care. The U.S. Supreme Court has said that "clear and convincing" evidence of an individual's wishes about medical care should be followed—even if they conflict with the wishes of close family members. (*Cruzan v. Director, Missouri Dept. of Health*, 497 U.S. 261 (1990).) A doctor who receives a properly signed and witnessed or notarized advance directive has a duty either to honor its instructions, or to make sure the patient is transferred to the care of another doctor who will honor them.

When you make your advance directive, you can say as much or as little as you wish about the kind of health care you want to receive. Some people don't say anything at all; they just use their advance directive to name an agent who will make all medical decisions for them if they become incapacitated. For example, you can leave it to your agent to direct all of your medical care, including decisions about life-prolonging treatment if you were ever close to death from a terminal illness or in a permanent coma. But if you want to control your own

health care to the greatest possible extent, you can write out detailed instructions about the kind of care you want (this chapter shows you how) and name someone to oversee and enforce your directions.

Before you jump into preparing your advance directive, however, you'll want to understand some basic facts about the document. This section explains:

- who can make an advance directive
- when your advance directive takes effect
- the duty of medical personnel to honor your directive, and
- when your advance directive ends.

PODCAST

Learn by listening. Visit Nolo's website to hear a podcast on the subject of living wills and medical directives, see Appendix A for the link.

Who Can Make an Advance Directive

You must be at least 18 years old to make a valid document directing your health care. You must also be of sound mind—that is, able to understand what the document means, what it contains, and how it works. For a more detailed discussion of this requirement, see "The Mental Capacity Requirement" in Chapter 1.

When Your Advance Directive Takes Effect

Unless you specify otherwise, your advance directive takes effect only if your primary physician someday determines that you lack the ability, or capacity, to make your own health care decisions. (Cal. Prob. Code § 4701.) Lacking capacity means that:

- you can't understand the nature and consequences of the health care choices that are available to you (including significant benefits, risks, and alternatives), and

- you are unable to communicate your wishes for care, whether orally, in writing, or through gestures. (Cal. Prob. Code § 4609.)

Practically speaking, this means that if you are so ill or injured that you cannot express your health care wishes in any way, your documents will spring immediately into effect. If, however, there is some question about your ability to understand your treatment choices and communicate clearly, your doctor will decide whether it's time for your advance directive to become operative.

If you want to give your agent authority to manage your health care immediately, however, you have that option. All you have to do is check a box on your advance directive form that makes your agent's authority effective right away. You may prefer to make an immediately effective directive for any of several reasons, including:

Taking quick action. Your agent can put your document into effect as soon as he or she feels that you have lost the ability to make your own medical decisions. The agent will be able to make decisions for you without first having a doctor confirm that you are incapacitated. This may be particularly important if you are not under the care of a doctor with whom you have an established, trusting relationship.

Keeping control in the hands of your agent. You may feel that your agent is the best person to decide that you can no longer direct your own medical care. If so, you don't need to require the statement of a doctor.

Asking your agent to step in early. If you make your document effective right away, your agent can start making decisions for you whenever you decide that's what you want, even if you still have the capacity to make your own choices. If illness, exhaustion, or any other circumstances have left you feeling that you'd like someone you trust to deal with your doctors and make treatment choices for you, making an immediately effective document gives you that flexibility.

Making your document effective immediately will *not* give your agent the authority to override what you want in terms of treatment; you will always be able to dictate your own medical care if you have the ability to do so. And remember that even when you are no longer capable of making your own decisions, your agent must act in your best interests and try diligently to follow any health care wishes you've expressed in your advance directive or otherwise. (See "About Your Health Care Agent," below.)

Duty of Medical Personnel to Honor Your Advance Directive

Health care providers are generally required to comply with the wishes you set out in your advance directive, and to honor your agent's authority as long as the agent's directions are a reasonable interpretation of your wishes. (Cal. Prob. Code § 4733(a).) In some situations, however, a health care provider is permitted to reject a health care decision made by you or your agent. This is true when:

- the decision goes against the conscience of the individual health care provider (Cal. Prob. Code § 4734(a))
- the decision goes against a policy of a health care institution that is based on reasons of conscience, and that policy is promptly communicated to you or your agent (Cal. Prob. Code § 4734(b)), or
- the decision would lead to medically ineffective health care or health care that violates generally accepted health care standards applied by the health care provider or institution (Cal. Prob. Code § 4735).

But this doesn't mean that your advance directive can be ignored. A health care provider who refuses to comply with your wishes or the instructions of your agent must promptly inform you or your agent. If you or your agent wishes, the provider must immediately take steps to transfer you to another provider or institution that will honor your directive. The health care provider must continue to care for you until the transfer is complete. (Cal. Prob. Code § 4736.)

> EXAMPLE: Angie is a diabetic with serious kidney problems. She feels strongly that if she is close to death or in a permanent coma, she doesn't wish to receive any more life-sustaining treatment, including kidney dialysis or artificially administered food and water—and she prepares an advance health care directive saying so. When her condition suddenly worsens, she falls into a coma from which the doctors at the local hospital don't believe she will recover.
>
> When her agent seeks to enforce her health care wishes and discontinue life-prolonging care, the doctor in charge of her case balks, feeling especially uncomfortable about withholding nutritional fluids. But because the hospital itself does not have a policy against withholding these types of treatments, Angie's agent is able to transfer her case to another doctor who agrees to follow her directions.

If a health care provider improperly refuses to honor your wishes, your agent or any other concerned person can seek help from a court. A judge can compel the health care provider to comply with your instructions and recognize the authority of your agent. (Cal. Prob. Code § 4766(e).)

A health care provider who intentionally violates the laws discussed in this section may be legally liable for damages. Under California law, you could sue the provider for at least $2,500 and the cost of your attorneys' fees. (Cal. Prob. Code § 4742.)

When Your Advance Directive Ends

Your written wishes for health care remain effective as long as you are alive, unless you specifically revoke your advance directive or a court steps in. Court involvement is very rare.

You revoke your documents. You can change or revoke your advance directive at any time, as long as you are of sound mind. We explain how at the end of this chapter.

A court invalidates your documents. California law sensibly recognizes that a court is normally not the right place to make health care decisions. (Cal. Prob. Code § 4650.) However, if your health care is the subject of a dispute and someone questions the validity of your advance directive, the matter may end up before a judge.

If someone doubts that you had the mental capacity to prepare a legally valid advance directive, that person can ask a court to invalidate your document. (See Cal. Prob. Code §§ 4765, 4766.) Such lawsuits are rare, but they do sometimes occur. The burden of proving that you were not of sound mind when you made your advance directive falls on the person who challenges the validity of your document. The law presumes that you had the mental capacity to make your advance directive. (Cal. Prob. Code § 4657.)

 SEE AN EXPERT

Preventing others from challenging your advance directive. If you have reason to believe that specific people in your life may strongly object to your health care wishes, you can use your advance directive to prevent them from filing a court petition to invalidate your document. To do this, you must name the individuals in your directive and obtain a signed statement from a lawyer, confirming that the lawyer has advised you about your legal options. There are certain rights you can't restrict— for example, your health care agent will always be permitted to petition a court concerning your mental capacity or to determine whether your advance directive has taken effect. (Cal. Prob. Code § 4753.) To learn more, consult a qualified California estate planning lawyer.

How Pregnancy May Affect Your Advance Directive

There is one situation in which your specific directions about health care might be challenged or ignored completely: when you are pregnant. While California law does not specifically limit the effect of your advance directive if you are pregnant, if you may become pregnant, it's a good idea to explicitly state what you want if your advance directive goes into effect while you are carrying a child. You can choose that your documents:

- be given no effect during pregnancy, or
- be carried out as written.

We show you how to do this in "Directing Health Care for Different Situations," below.

If you specify that the health care wishes in your advance directive be given no effect, your agent or health care providers will have the discretion to decide what care is appropriate. They are most likely to administer whatever life-prolonging procedures are available—particularly if the fetus is at least four or five months old, potentially viable, and unharmed by your condition.

If you choose that your health care directions be carried out as written if you are pregnant, you may meet some resistance from doctors and hospitals. This is particularly true if you direct that life-prolonging treatment, pain medication, or food and water should be withheld. And you are more apt to run into resistance the more advanced your pregnancy becomes. If you are into the second trimester—the fourth through sixth months—doctors are likely to administer all medical care they deem necessary to keep you and the fetus alive.

By the third trimester of a pregnancy—the seventh through ninth months—it may be practically impossible to dictate that doctors withhold life-prolonging medical care. And doctors who balk at enforcing your contrary wishes have some legal support for ignoring you and administering all available care. Doctors can argue that while individuals may have the right to direct their own health care, they have no right to direct that care for another living being, arguably—under the U.S. Supreme Court's decision in *Roe v. Wade*, 401 U.S. 113 (1973)—a fetus six months old or older.

It is also possible that a court could invalidate your document if it wasn't properly witnessed or notarized (for more information about these requirements, see "Making Your Advance Directive Legal," below). If this happens, however, it is still likely that any wishes for health care you set out in the document will be followed—as long as they are clearly expressed and you were of sound mind when you wrote them down. In the famous *Cruzan* case, the U.S. Supreme Court said that any strong evidence of someone's wishes for care should be honored: Your directions won't be ignored simply because of a technical error.

A court revokes your agent's authority. If, after your document takes effect, someone believes that your agent is not acting according to your wishes or in your best interests, the concerned person can go to court and ask for an investigation of your agent's behavior.

If a court finds that your agent is acting improperly and revokes his or her authority, the job will go first to an alternate agent you named in your advance directive. If there is no available alternate (or if the court invalidates your entire document for one of the reasons discussed just above) a conservator will be appointed to make health care decisions for you. When naming a conservator, a court will consider the following people, in this order:

- your spouse or registered domestic partner
- an adult child
- a parent, or
- a sibling.

If one of the people on this list doesn't want to take the job of conservator, that person has the power to nominate someone else to take the position before the court moves on to the next person on the priority list. (Cal. Prob. Code § 1812.)

You get a divorce or terminate your domestic partnership. Getting divorced has no effect on your written directions for health care. But if you named your spouse as your health care agent, his or her authority is automatically revoked when the divorce is final. (Cal. Prob. Code § 4697.) If you named an alternate agent in your advance directive, that person will take over.

If you get a divorce after you make an advance directive, it's wise to eliminate confusion by starting over. Even if you named an alternate, make a new document and name someone else as your agent.

If you are a member of a registered domestic partnership, the same concern applies to you. If you formally end your partnership, be sure to make a new document and name a new health care agent.

After your death. Your advance directive remains effective after your death only for some very limited purposes. Your agent can supervise the disposition of your body, including authorizing an autopsy or organ donation, unless you specifically withhold these powers when you make your advance directive. (You'll learn more about this below.)

About Your Health Care Agent

One of the most important benefits of making an advance health care directive is that you get to choose someone to supervise your medical care if you are unable to do so yourself. This person is usually called your agent, but occasionally goes by "attorney-in-fact."

You can give your agent a great deal of control over your medical decisions, or very little. But it's almost always a good idea to name an agent, even if that person will be charged only with enforcing the detailed health care wishes you express in your advance directive. Your agent can make sure medical personnel know of your preferences, lobby on your behalf to get them enforced, and if necessary, go to court to be sure you get the care you want.

If you don't name an agent, health care providers may not follow your wishes as diligently as they would if an agent were present. And without an agent, if doctors have questions about the kind of care you should receive, they will turn to your close family members for guidance. This will probably be fine if the person they ask is the same person you would have named as your agent—your spouse, say, or one of your grown children—and no one else who is close to you strongly disagrees with what they decide. But if your loved ones don't agree about your care, they may have to ask a court for the authority to make health care decisions for you or to enforce the wishes you've expressed. You can prevent these difficulties by using your advance directive to name a trusted person to represent you.

EXAMPLE: A California case illustrates the vital importance of making an advance directive and naming a health care agent. Robert Wendland was in his mid-thirties when he was severely injured in a car accident. He was in a coma for more than a year before he awakened into a state that some doctors have described as "minimally conscious." Although awake, he was severely brain-damaged and paralyzed on his right side. Six months after Robert came out of the coma, his wife Rose, who had been named Robert's conservator, decided to withhold food and fluids, saying that Robert had earlier told her and other family members that he wouldn't want to live in a state of total dependence. Robert had not, however, prepared an advance directive. Robert's doctors supported Rose's decision. However, when Robert's mother and sister learned of Rose's plans, they went to court and obtained a temporary restraining order to stop her, asserting that Robert would have wanted to be kept alive. Thus began a bitter family fight, with both sides claiming they knew what was best for Robert and battling to be named his permanent conservator. Eight years after Robert's accident, the family was still fighting.

Robert died of pneumonia in July of 2001; a month later, the Supreme Court of California ruled that conservators cannot terminate life support for conscious—though severely disabled—people without clear and convincing evidence of their wishes. (*Conservatorship of Wendland*, 110 Cal.Rptr.2d 412 (Cal. 2001).)

Your Agent's Powers

As mentioned just above, you can give your agent as much or as little power as feels comfortable to you. Most people give their agent comprehensive power to supervise their care. Recognizing this, California's advance directive form gives the person you name the power to make all health care decisions for you unless you specifically limit that authority in the document. Unless you expressly restrict your agent's authority, your agent will have the power to:

- consent or refuse consent to any medical treatment that affects your physical or mental health, with a few exceptions (discussed in the next section)
- hire or fire medical personnel and make decisions about the best medical facilities for you
- approve or disapprove diagnostic tests, surgical procedures, or medications
- direct the provision, withholding, or withdrawal of artificial nutrition and hydration and all other forms of life-

sustaining medical care, including cardiopulmonary resuscitation (CPR), and
- make anatomical gifts, authorize an autopsy, and direct the disposition of your body after death.

Again, keep in mind that as long as you are able to understand and communicate your own wishes, your agent cannot override what you want. Your agent steps in only if you can no longer manage on your own.

Of course, if you also use your advance directive to specify what type of care you want to receive, your agent is legally bound to follow your wishes, as are medical care providers. And you can restrict your agent's authority even further if you wish, by stating that it is strictly limited to enforcing whatever wishes you express. We show you how to place restrictions on your agent's authority below.

HIPAA: What You Need to Know When Making Your Advance Directive

If you've recently visited a doctor, you know there's a law that requires patients to sign forms regarding medical privacy and the release of medical information. This federal law is called HIPAA, the Health Insurance Portability and Accountability Act. Some people have wondered whether it's necessary to prepare special HIPAA release forms to give a health care agent the authority to take over medical matters. In fact, this is not the case. When you make your advance directive, your agent is automatically authorized to obtain the medical information necessary to put your document into effect and carry out your wishes.

If, however, you make a durable power of attorney for finances, it may be necessary to prepare a HIPAA release so that document can take effect. We discuss this in detail in Chapter 4.

What Your Health Care Agent Can't Do

California law does not permit an agent to make certain medical decisions for you. Your agent may not:

- place you in a mental health facility (Cal. Prob. Code § 4652(a))
- authorize extreme psychiatric treatments, such as electroshock therapy (convulsive treatment), or psychiatric surgery (Cal. Prob. Code §§ 4652(b),(c))
- authorize sterilization or abortion (Cal. Prob. Code §§ 4652(d),(e))
- authorize, condone, or approve mercy killing (Cal. Prob. Code § 4653), or
- authorize any act that exceeds the limits you place on the agent in your advance directive (Cal. Prob. Code § 4681(a)).

For more information about assisted dying, see "Advance Directives and California's New Aid-in-Dying Law: What You Need to Know," in Chapter 1.

Your Health Care Agent's Legal Responsibilities

Your agent is required by law to follow any health care instructions you include in your advance directive, as well as any other wishes for treatment that the agent knows about. (Cal. Prob. Code § 4684.)

If your agent doesn't know what you would want in a given situation, the agent must make a decision for you based on what he or she believes to be in your best interests. When considering what would be best for you, your agent is required to consider all that he or she knows about your personal values and beliefs. For this reason, it's always a good idea to discuss your feelings about health care with your agent in addition to completing your advance directive.

EXAMPLE: Terrence prepares an advance directive appointing his partner, Susan, as his agent. He gives her the authority to make all medical decisions for him and doesn't write out any specific instructions in his advance directive. Several years later, Terrence is diagnosed with an aggressive form of colon cancer. In the months after his diagnosis, he and Susan have several long talks about the kind of care Terrence wants when he is close to death, as well as how he wants his body treated after death and what kind of memorial service he wants. As Terrence's death approaches, Susan attempts to follow Terrence's desires as much as possible, eventually lobbying his doctors to stop chemotherapy and other invasive treatments so that Terrence can die peacefully at home as he wished. After his death, she draws on their conversations to arrange for his burial and plan a small memorial gathering at the park near his childhood home.

Your agent is not permitted to make any decisions about your health care to which you object. (Cal. Prob. Code § 4689.) If your agent believes that you lack the ability to make medical decisions that are in your own best interest, he or she may ask a judge to step in, either to enforce the wishes you set out in your own advance directive or, if you expressed no wishes, to allow your agent to make a decision despite your objection. (See Cal. Prob. Code §§ 4765(d), 4766(a).)

Choosing Your Health Care Agent

The person you name as your health care agent should be someone you trust absolutely— and someone with whom you feel confident discussing your wishes. Your agent need not agree with your wishes for your medical care, but must completely respect your right to get the kind of treatment you want.

Your agent may be your spouse or partner, relative, or close friend. Keep in mind that your agent may have to fight to assert your wishes in the face of a stubborn medical establishment—and against the wishes of family members who may be driven by their own beliefs and interests, rather than yours. If you foresee the possibility of a conflict in enforcing your wishes, be sure to choose an agent who is strong-willed and assertive.

While you need not name someone who lives in the same city or state as you do, proximity is one factor to consider. If you have a long illness, your agent may be called upon to spend weeks or even months near your bedside, making sure medical personnel abide by your wishes for your medical treatment.

If you make a durable power of attorney for finances (see Chapter 4), it's usually wise to name the same person as both your agent for health care and your agent for finances. If you feel that you must name different people, be very sure you name agents who get along well and will be able to work together. You wouldn't, for example, want your agent for finances to interfere with your health care wishes by stalling or resisting payment of medical or insurance bills, two things over which your agent for finances will have control.

We show you how to name your agent in Part 1, below.

Naming More Than One Agent

Though you are legally permitted to name more than one person to represent you, you should name only one agent when you make your advance directive. This is true even if you know of two or more people who are suitable candidates and who agree to undertake the job together. There may be problems, brought on by passing time and human nature, with naming people to share the job. In the critical time during which they would be overseeing your wishes and directing your care, they might disagree, rendering them ineffective as lobbyists on your behalf. Feuding agents could even end up settling their dispute in court, further delaying and confusing your care.

If you fear that those close to you may feel hurt if you name someone else to represent you, take some time to talk with them to explain your choice. Or, if there are several people you'd feel comfortable naming, you might even let them decide among themselves who the agent will be. If you approve of their choice, you can accept it—and name the others as alternate agents in case your first choice can't serve.

> **CAUTION**
> **Don't name a health care provider as your agent.** California law prohibits the following people from serving as an agent under an advance directive:
> - your treating health care provider or an employee of the health care institution where you are receiving care, unless the employee is related to you (or is your registered domestic partner) or you and the employee both work for the health care institution
> - an operator of a community care facility— for example, a residential rehabilitation or counseling center
> - an employee of a community care facility, unless the employee is related to you (or is your registered domestic partner) or you and the employee both work at the community care facility
> - an operator of a residential care facility for the elderly, or
> - an employee of a residential care facility for the elderly, unless the employee is related to you (or is your registered domestic partner) or you also work at the residential care facility.
> (Cal. Prob. Code § 4659.)

Naming an Alternate Agent

California's advance directive form permits you to name one or two alternate agents to represent you if your first choice is unable to take the job for any reason or resigns after your advance directive takes effect. Alternates serve one at a time, in the order that you specify.

It's a good idea to name at least one alternate agent, but you should be as thoughtful about naming your alternates as you are about your first choice: Be sure to name people who will represent you well if the need arises.

We show you how to name alternate agents in Part 1, below.

If You Do Not Name a Health Care Agent

If you do not know of anyone you trust to oversee your medical care, it's not necessary to name an agent. In fact, it is better not to name anyone than to name someone who is not comfortable with the directions you leave—or who is not likely to assert your wishes strongly.

But even if you don't name an agent, you should still complete the rest of the advance directive, stating your health care directions. Even without an agent, medical personnel are required to follow your written wishes for health care—or to find someone who will care for you in the way you have directed. If you do not name a health care agent, be certain to discuss your wishes for medical care with a doctor or hospital representative likely to be involved in providing that care.

Preparing Your Advance Directive

This book offers the California advance health care directive form as a tear-out form in Appendix B or as a free download from Nolo's website. (See Appendix A for a link to the downloadable form.) If you download the form, you can complete it with your word processing program, following the instructions below.

If you choose the tear-out form, begin by making a few photocopies of the blank form. You can use one for a draft and save a clean one for the final document—the one you will sign and have notarized or witnessed. It's fine to fill in the blanks by hand. Be sure to print legibly and use black ink. Don't erase, white out, or cross out anything in your form, unless the document specifically states that you may cross out words. If you are directed to cross out something, keep it simple: Draw a straight line through the unwanted text.

This section takes you through the form one part at a time. There's a sample form at the end, so you can see what a filled-in form looks like. Keep in mind, however, that depending on your wishes, your completed form may look different from the sample.

Part 1: Power of Attorney for Health Care

Part 1 of the advance directive is called your power of attorney for health care. This is where you:

- name the primary and alternate agents who will make health care decisions for you if you are unable to do so yourself (or if you choose not to)
- place any limits on the powers you want your agent to have under your advance directive, and
- indicate whether you want your agent's authority to take effect immediately or only after a doctor finds that you are incapacitated.

(1) Designation of Agent

Begin by filling in your own name and address in the first two blanks of the form. Then enter the complete name, address, and phone numbers of your first-choice agent on the next several lines. It's important to include correct phone numbers; health care providers should be able to make quick contact with your agent if necessary. If a number changes later, it's okay to write the new number into the form. Be sure to notify anyone who has a copy of your document that your agent's phone number has changed.

After you name your agent, you can name up to two alternate agents by entering their names and contact information in the next two sets of lines. You should appoint at least one alternate if you know someone you trust enough to take the job. (See "Naming an Alternate Agent," above.)

(2) Agent's Authority

After you name your agent and alternates, Section (2) of Part 1 gives you the opportunity to place limits on their authority to make medical decisions. Any limits you set will apply to your agent and alternate agents alike. If you do not place any restrictions, your agent will have broad powers, as discussed in "Your Agent's Powers," above.

As you consider your agent's powers, keep in mind that in Part 2 of the advance directive, you will be asked to enter your specific health care instructions, if any, and that your agent is required to follow these instructions. You do not need to enter your instructions twice by placing corresponding restrictions on your agent here. For example, if you will state in Part 2 that you do not wish to receive life-prolonging medical treatment at the end of your life, you do not have to use this part of the form to forbid your agent to authorize such treatment.

So what kind of restrictions might you want to include here? One might be to give your agent only the authority to carry out the health care wishes you specify in your advance directive, and not to make other medical decisions for you. If that's what you want, you can add a paragraph like this one:

> My agent's authority is limited to supervising and enforcing the wishes for medical care that I have expressed in this advance directive. My agent may take all actions on my behalf that are necessary to enforce my written wishes.

But think carefully before you add limiting language to your document. One of the most important reasons for appointing a health care agent is so that he or she can respond to your situation as it develops. Your medical needs may change in ways that you cannot now foresee, and an agent who has full power can act for you no matter what the circumstances.

Giving Your Agent Power to Decide Where You Will Live

At some point, you may need to move from your own home into a home or facility where you can receive ongoing medical or personal care. California law lets you give your health care agent the power to decide where you will live. If you don't give your agent this power and don't specify any wishes about your residence, your loved ones will have to work out this decision if the issue ever comes up.

If you want to give your health care agent authority to decide where you will live, add a paragraph like one of these to your document:

> My agent may determine where I will live.

> Though I wish to remain at home as long as possible, if my agent determines that I am no longer able to reside at home, then my agent may choose where I will live.

> My agent may determine where I will live. However, if I must move to a nursing facility, I would prefer the Hilldale Home on Orange Street in San Rafael.

(3) When Agent's Authority Becomes Effective

Check the box in Section (3) of the form if you wish to make your agent's authority effective immediately. (See "When Your Advance Directive Takes Effect," above.)

(4) Agent's Obligation

You don't have to do anything in Section (4) of the form. This paragraph simply restates your agent's duties under the law: to follow your instructions and make decisions in your best interest.

(5) Agent's Authority to Make Post-Death Decisions

Unless you state otherwise in Section (5), your agent will have the power to make anatomical gifts, authorize an autopsy, and direct the disposition of your body after death. You will have the opportunity to state your specific wishes about organ donation in Part 3 of the advance directive—and your agent must follow your directions. If you want to place any additional limits on your agent's authority, enter them on the blank lines in this section. Here are a few examples:

> My agent may not authorize the donation of any of my organs, tissues, or body parts after death.

> After death, I do not want my body to be embalmed. I prefer that my body be cremated.

> I direct that my agent follow the instructions in the attached letter directing the disposition of my body and other final arrangements.

The expenses of carrying out your final arrangements—services, cremation or burial, and the like—are usually paid from funds you leave at your death. If there isn't enough money in your estate when you die, your close family members will be expected to pay after-death costs. Your health care agent is liable for these costs only if your agent specifically agrees to pay them, or if the agent makes specific decisions resulting in reasonable costs that your own funds are unable to cover. (Cal. Health & Safety Code § 7100.)

Stating Your Wishes for Final Arrangements

Letting your survivors know in detail what kind of body disposition and ceremonies you envision saves them the pain of making such decisions at what is likely to be a difficult time for them. And planning some of these details in advance can help save money, too. Wise comparison shopping—for mortuary services, a coffin, urn, gravesite, or other after-death needs—can keep costs reasonable.

The best way to give direction to your loved ones about your wishes for final arrangements is to write them down in a letter, providing as much detail as you can. You can give the letter to your loved ones, and attach it to your advance directive if you like.

For more information and for help making your decisions and plans, see "Making Final Arrangements," the bonus guide that you can download from the Nolo website (see Appendix A for the link).

---

(6) Nomination of Conservator

If a court ever needs to appoint a conservator (see "When Your Advance Directive Ends," above) to oversee your medical decisions and arrange for your personal care (clothing, food, and shelter), Section (6) of the advance directive automatically nominates your health care agent for that position. If your agent is not willing or available to act as your conservator, your document nominates your alternate agents, in the order named. This is what most people want, because in selecting an agent and alternates they have already given much thought to choosing the best person to act.

If you do not wish to include this nomination in your form for some reason, you can delete the entire clause—using your word processing program if you are completing the downloadable form, or by completely crossing out and then initialing the clause if you are using the tear-out version.

Part 2: Instructions for Health Care

Because health care directives sprang from the Right to Die movement, many people tend to think of them as documents appropriate only for directing that life-prolonging procedures be withdrawn or withheld. However, an advance directive is really a way to direct doctors to give you whatever type of medical care you want, within reality and reason. For example, some people want to reinforce that they would like to receive all medical treatment that is available—and an advance directive is the proper place to specify that.

(7) End-of-Life Decisions

In Section (7), the California advance directive asks you to state your preferences about life-prolonging treatments or procedures when you are at the end of your life. Basically, the form gives you two choices: You can request that you be kept alive as long as possible, or that your life not be prolonged in certain end-of-life situations. You can supplement these choices by writing in your own instructions in Section (9) of your advance directive. (See below.)

This section briefly discusses and defines medical procedures that are most often deemed "life prolonging." It's best if you at least read quickly through the definitions so that you understand your choices. However, if

you already know you want to direct that all procedures be provided—or that all procedures be withheld—you can skip these definitions and simply check the box in this section that indicates your preference:

- Check box (a) if you do not wish to receive life-prolonging treatment. This means that your life will not be prolonged if you (1) have an incurable and irreversible condition that will result in your death within a relatively short time, (2) are in a permanent coma, or (3) are seriously ill such that, in the opinion of your agent, the likely risks to you of treatment would outweigh the benefits you might receive.
- Check box (b) if you do wish to receive life-prolonging treatment. This means that doctors must prolong your life as long as possible, no matter how poor the prognosis, within the limits of generally accepted health care standards.

It Doesn't Get More Personal Than This

For many people, the desire to direct what kind of medical care they want to receive is driven by a very specific event—watching a loved one die, having an unsatisfactory brush with the medical establishment, or preparing for serious surgery.

Your ultimate decisions about medical treatment are likely to be influenced by factors such as your medical history, your knowledge of other people's experiences with life-prolonging medical procedures, or your religious beliefs. If you are having difficulty deciding about your preferences for medical care, take some time to consider what's getting in your way. If you are unsure about the meaning or specifics of a particular medical treatment, turn to a doctor you trust for a more complete explanation. If the impediment is fear of sickness or death, you might talk over your feelings with family members and friends.

If you are not sure what you want, read about the treatments listed below and consider how you feel about receiving them when you are close to death. Bear in mind that the available medical procedures will change over time. Technological advances mean that currently unfathomable procedures and treatments will become available, and treatments that are now common will become obsolete. Also, the treatments that are available vary drastically by region, depending on the sophistication and funding levels of local medical facilities.

When completing your advance directive, the best that you can do is to become familiar with the kinds of medical procedures that are most commonly administered to patients who are seriously ill. The best that we can do is to provide you with clear explanations. Both will help you produce an advance directive that accurately reflects your wishes.

Transfusions of blood and blood products. Partial or full blood transfusions may be recommended to combat diseases that impair the blood system, to foster healing after a blood loss, or to replenish blood lost through surgery, disease, or injury. "Blood products" means different components of blood: fluids (called plasma) and blood cells.

Cardiopulmonary resuscitation (CPR). Cardio-pulmonary resuscitation is used when a person's heart or breathing has stopped. CPR includes applying physical pressure and using mouth-to-mouth resuscitation. Electrical shocks are also used if available. CPR is often accompanied by intravenous drugs used to normalize body systems. A final step in CPR is often attaching the patient to a respirator to help breathing. A respirator may be temporary, though some patients—those in a coma, for example—may be kept on a respirator until the end of life.

Diagnostic tests. Diagnostic tests are commonly used to evaluate urine, blood, and other body fluids and to check on all bodily functions. Diagnostic tests can include X-rays and more sophisticated tests of brainwaves or other internal body systems. Some diagnostic tests—including surgery—can be expensive and invasive, producing pain and other side effects.

Dialysis. A dialysis machine is used to clean and add essential substances to the blood—through tubes placed in blood vessels or into the abdomen—when kidneys do not function properly. The entire cleansing process takes three or more hours and is performed on most dialysis patients two to three times a week. With portable dialysis machines, some dialysis patients can perform the procedure at home themselves, rather than in a hospital or another facility.

Administration of drugs. The most common and most controversial drugs given to seriously ill or comatose patients are antibiotics—administered by mouth, through a feeding tube, or by injection. Antibiotics are used to arrest and squelch infectious diseases. Patients in very weakened conditions may not respond even to massive doses of antibiotics.

Many health care providers argue that infections can actually be a benefit to those in advanced stages of an illness, since they may render a patient unconscious, and presumably not in pain, or help to speed the dying process. Others contend that if an antibiotic can eliminate symptoms of an illness, it is almost always the proper medical treatment.

Drugs may also be used to eliminate or alleviate pain. When completing your advance directive, you can give specific instructions about pain medication in Section (8). (See below.)

Use of a respirator. A mechanical respirator or ventilator assists or takes over breathing for a patient by pumping air in and out of the lungs. These machines dispense a regulated amount of air into the lungs at a set rate—and periodically purge the lungs. Patients are connected to respirators either by a tube that goes through the mouth and throat into the lung or attaches directly to the lung surgically.

Respirators are often used to stabilize patients who are suffering from an acute trauma or breathing crisis. Once a patient has been attached to a respirator, most doctors will resist removing the machinery because of the risk of the patient's death, unless there is clear written direction that the patient does not wish to remain on a respirator.

Surgery. Surgical procedures such as amputation are sometimes used to stem the spread of life-threatening infections or to keep vital organs functioning. Major surgery, such as a heart bypass, may also be performed on patients who are terminally ill or comatose. You might want to consider the cost, time spent recovering from the invasive surgery, and the ultimate prognosis in deciding whether to include surgery in your final medical treatment.

(8) Relief From Pain

California's advance directive form assumes that you want relief from pain and discomfort at all times, even if pain medication hastens your death. Section (8) specifically states that you want to receive treatment that alleviates pain, no matter what your other wishes for care. If you prefer, however, you may modify or change these instructions by entering your wishes on the blank lines in Section (8). For example, you may wish to specify that you do not want particular types of pain drugs. Or, you may state that you do not want so much pain medication that it compromises your ability to remain alert and aware of your loved ones. Here are a few sample statements to help you phrase such requests:

> I do not want to receive any types or amounts of pain medication that may cause me to hallucinate.

> If I am no longer able to communicate my wishes for care, I would like my health care agent to have a detailed discussion with my doctor to establish a plan to keep me free from pain and anxiety. I do not mind receiving a mild dose of antidepressants or morphine, but would like as much as possible to be aware of my surroundings and visitors.

> Even if I am experiencing intense pain, I want to occasionally be aware of my family's presence if that is possible. If that means reducing the amount of pain medication every couple of days so I can be with them, that is what I want.

(9) Other Wishes

In Section (9) of the advance directive, you can provide any additional instructions for your health care. You don't need to use this section if you feel that the previous provisions accurately and completely state your wishes, but if you have more to say, this is the place to do it.

Individual health care instructions are virtually unlimited in their scope and the way they can be written. Here, we discuss just some of the additions and modifications that you may wish to make. If there are specific issues that concern you and aren't covered here, talk to your doctor.

Artificially Administered Food and Water

If you cannot communicate to others your preferences for your own health care, it is also likely that you will not be able to voluntarily take in water or food through your mouth. Unless you indicate that treatment should be withheld, doctors will provide you with a mix of nutrients and fluids through tubes inserted in a vein, into your stomach through your nose, or directly into your stomach through a surgical incision, depending on your condition.

Intravenous (IV) feeding, where fluids are introduced through a vein in an arm or a leg, is a short-term procedure. Tube feeding, however, can be carried on indefinitely.

Permanently unconscious patients can sometimes live for years with artificial feeding and hydration without regaining consciousness. If food and water are removed, death will occur in a relatively short time due to dehydration, rather than starvation. Such a course of action generally includes a plan of medication to keep the patient comfortable.

When you prepare your advance directive, it's a good idea to make clear your wishes about artificially administered nutrition and hydration, by using a statement like one of the following:

Regardless of my condition, it is my desire to receive nutrition and hydration in all ways possible.

If I have any of the conditions listed in Section (7) of this advance directive, I do not wish to receive nutrition and hydration by any artificial means.

If I have any of the conditions listed in Section (7) of this advance directive, I do not wish to receive nutrition and hydration by any artificial means unless it is necessary for my comfort or to alleviate pain.

I do not want artificial nutrition and hydration under any circumstances except for the treatment of a temporary condition in which I am unable to eat or drink and then only for a short time. If, within a short period (as determined by my agent after consulting my physician), there is no benefit to me, then I instruct that artificial nutrition and hydration be withdrawn.

Decisions about food and water are difficult for many people. Keep in mind that as long as you are able to communicate your wishes, by whatever means, you will not be denied food and water if you want it.

RESOURCE

Where to get more help. If you are not sure whether or not you would want to receive artificially administered food and water, you may wish to talk with your doctor or do some more research on your own. The following book is a good resource that may help you sort out your feelings about the issue: *Hard Choices for Loving People: CPR, Feeding Tubes, Palliative Care, Comfort Measures, and the Patient with a Serious Illness*, by Hank Dunn (A & A Publishers). This well-written resource features a good discussion of the issues surrounding artificial nutrition and hydration, exploring the various medical, religious and philosophical views on the subject. Learn more at www.hardchoices.com.

Specific Instructions

In addition to considering artificially administered food and water, you may have strong feelings about other medical care you want to receive, for any number of reasons. You may have watched someone close to you either suffer terribly or miraculously improve as the result of a particular kind of care, such as prolonged attachment to a respirator or the administration of antibiotics. You may have moral objections to either receiving or withholding certain types of treatments. Or perhaps you are quite up-to-date on medical technology and the advantages and disadvantages of various procedures and medications and wish to dictate your care based on your understanding of what's medically most appropriate. Here are a few examples of the types of statements you can add to your form:

Although I have indicated that I do not wish to receive life-prolonging treatment, if I have any of the conditions listed in Section (7) of this advance directive, I want to receive any drug therapies that my primary physician recommends.

Although I have indicated that I wish to receive life-prolonging treatment, if I have any of the conditions listed in Section (7) of this advance directive, I do not wish to receive CPR or to remain on a respirator for longer than one week.

Although I have indicated that I wish to receive life-prolonging treatment, if I have any of the conditions listed in Section (7) of this advance directive, I do not wish to receive surgical treatment.

Directing Health Care for Different Situations

If you don't feel comfortable checking the box rejecting life-prolonging treatment in the circumstances listed, you may prefer to specify the kinds of care you want to receive in different situations. For example, someone facing the diagnosis of a terminal illness may feel that the best medical care under such circumstances would be to have as much pain and suffering alleviated as possible through drugs and IVs, without any heroic medical maneuvers, such as invasive surgery or additional painful diagnostic tests.

But the same person considering treatment for a permanent coma may choose to hold out hope for the possibility of some medical cure for the condition—and direct that all possible medical treatments be administered if they become comatose. Or that person may feel strongly that life in a coma would completely lack meaning—and direct that all medical procedures, including food, water, and pain medication, be discontinued.

Here are some samples on which you might model your directions:

If I am diagnosed with an incurable injury, disease, or illness and if the application of life-sustaining procedures would serve only to artificially prolong the moment of my death, then I desire that all life-prolonging treatment be withheld or removed. However, I wish to continue to receive pain medication, nutrition, and hydration until my death.

If I have been in a coma for at least one week and two qualified physicians familiar with my condition have diagnosed the coma as irreversible, then I desire that all life-sustaining treatment—including nutrition, hydration, and pain medication—be removed or withheld.

If I am diagnosed to be in a permanent coma, I want my life to be prolonged for as long as possible.

If in my agent's judgment the risks and burdens to me of the proposed treatment outweigh the expected benefits, then I desire that all life-prolonging treatment be withheld or withdrawn. I desire that my agent consider relief from suffering, preservation or restoration of functioning, and the quality as well as the extent of my life when making decisions concerning life-prolonging treatment.

If I develop Alzheimer's disease, I would like all noninvasive life-prolonging treatments, such as artificial nutrition, fluids, and antibiotics, as long as I have the ability to meaningfully interact with my family and friends, but I do not want highly intrusive treatments such as CPR, a respirator, or kidney dialysis. However, if I lose the capacity for meaningful interaction, I want only treatments that will make me more comfortable and free from pain. I would then not want artificial hydration or nutrition or antibiotics.

> I do not wish to receive life-prolonging treatment if I am unable to live at home.

> I do not wish to have life-saving surgery performed if two licensed physicians familiar with my condition determine that I will never be able to walk or talk again.

If You Might Become Pregnant

If there is a chance you might be pregnant when your advance directive takes effect, this is the place to state whether or not you want your health care wishes to be carried out as written. Here are some clauses to help you write out your wishes:

> If I am pregnant, I direct that my wishes for health care be given no effect during the course of my pregnancy.

> If I am pregnant, I direct that my wishes for health care be given no effect if my primary physician believes that the fetus can develop to the point of live birth. Otherwise, I direct that my wishes for health care be carried out as written.

> If I am pregnant, I direct that my wishes for health care be carried out as written.

For a discussion of the possible effects of pregnancy on your advance directive, see "How Pregnancy May Affect Your Advance Directive," near the beginning of this chapter.

Palliative Care

As discussed above, Section (8) of the advance directive addresses your wishes for pain relief. In addition to traditional treatments for relieving pain, you may want to think about other types of treatment to keep you comfortable. Care to keep you pain-free and comfortable is often called "palliative care."

Rather than focusing on a cure or prolonging life, palliative care emphasizes quality of life and dignity by helping a patient to remain comfortable and free from pain until life ends naturally.

Studies have shown that palliative care services are greatly appreciated by the families and friends of dying patients. Numerous organizations promote public awareness of palliative care options, and information about treatment options is widely available on the Internet. (See below.) However, despite the wide recognition of the benefits of palliative care, studies have revealed that relatively few people get the palliative care they should. Many hospitals do not have integrated palliative care plans among their treatment options. Few doctors understand it well, and medical training programs are still in the early stages of developing and offering palliative care education for future health care providers. As a result, many people die in hospital intensive care units, sometimes in great pain, not knowing how their suffering could have been eased. You may wish to spend some time educating yourself about palliative care so that you can discuss your wishes with your health care agent and your treatment providers. In your advance directive, you can make any statements you wish about your desires for palliative care. Here is an example:

> During the final days of my life, I would like to have my loved ones with me as much as possible. Please feel free to hold my hand, talk gently with me, sing to me, or just sit quietly nearby. My favorite books of poetry are on my bedside table and I would appreciate being read to from those.

RESOURCE

More information about palliative care. There are many resources to help you understand your options when it comes to palliative care. To learn more, you may want to start with Get Palliative Care (getpalliativecare.org), a comprehensive website developed and maintained by the Center to Advance Palliative Care (CAPC). The following books may also be useful:

- *Care at the Close of Life: Evidence and Experience*, by Stephen McPhee, Margaret A. Winker, Michael W. Rabow, Steven Z. Pantilat and Amy J. Markowitz (McGraw-Hill Professional)
- *Final Gifts: Understanding the Special Aware-ness, Needs, and Communications of the Dying*, by Maggie Callanan and Patricia Kelley (Bantam)
- *Handbook for Mortals: Guidance for People Facing Serious Illness*, by Joanne Lynn, M.D., and Joan Harrold, M.D. (Oxford University Press)

Location of Care

If where you receive care in the final months, weeks, or days of your life is very important to you, you can use your advance directive to set out your wishes. You may state a specific location that you would prefer, such as "at home" or at a particular hospital or hospice facility. Or, you may want to make a more general statement of your preferences, such as any location that lets you be with loved ones at all times.

On the other hand, you may wish to make clear that the location of your care is not as important as getting the treatment you desire. Perhaps you feel that if getting the care you want means being in the intensive care unit of a hospital, you would want to be there. You can state that whatever it takes to prolong your life is more important than where your care is administered.

Location of care may also arise as an issue surrounding diseases such as Alzheimer's or other types of severe dementia. If you have preferences regarding nursing homes or other long-term care options, you may say so.

When specifying wishes for the location of your care, be mindful of creating possible inconsistencies with other health care instructions you have given. For example, if you've expressed a wish for continuation of life-prolonging treatments during a terminal illness, and you've also expressed a preference to receive care at home, make clear which factor is more important. That is, are you willing to forgo some care in order to remain at home, or does the availability of life-sustaining treatment trump your concern about location?

Most important, don't forget to discuss your feelings and wishes with your doctor, your health care agent (if you have named one), and other loved ones.

Here are a couple of samples to help you express your wishes about the location of your care:

> If possible, I would like to remain at home at the end of my life, even if doing so means I cannot receive types of life-prolonging care that are available only in a hospital setting.

> If I have to be hospitalized at the end of my life, I would prefer to be taken to Mountain View General, where I have received excellent care in the past.

Personal or Religious Values

At the end of life, health care issues inevitably arise that are not covered by specific directions. When that happens, a statement of your overall philosophy or religious beliefs on matters of medical treatment and dying can help your care providers make decisions on your behalf.

This can be a difficult subject to address, but you may want to consider topics such as:

- your overall goals for your health care
- any fears that you have
- your spiritual or religious beliefs or traditions

- your beliefs about when life would no longer be worth living, and
- your thoughts about how your medical condition may affect your family—personally, practically, financially, or otherwise.

Certainly, you should not feel obligated to write a treatise on these matters in your health care directive. If you have any particularly strong feelings, however, they are worth noting. You should also make a particular point to discuss these issues with your health care agent and other loved ones.

Following are a couple of brief examples of personal statements:

> I have written a detailed letter to my health care agent that expresses my personal feelings about death and dying. It is in the top drawer of my bedside table. I would like my agent to open the letter and read it to close family members and friends if I am no longer able to speak for myself.

> Even though I have expressed a wish to be kept alive as long as possible, I do not wish my medical care to become a financial or emotional burden to my children. I know that you will do all you can to care for me and keep me comfortable, but if my care begins to cause undue exhaustion or anxiety, or if it begins to drain your personal financial resources, I want you to discontinue any heroic measures to keep me alive—including a respirator or artificially administered food and water if I am permanently unconscious.

Part 3: Donation of Organs at Death

Part 3 of the advance directive allows you to state whether you want to donate any of your organs, tissues, or body parts after you die. This decision is, of course, a very personal matter. Here's some information that may help you decide whether or not you want to be a donor.

The Need for Donated Organs

Many Californians are in dire need of organ transplants. More than 22,000 people in this state (about 120,000 nationwide) are currently waiting for life-saving organ transplant surgery—and based on current rates of donation, one in three of them will die before receiving a transplant. Although the number of organ donations in California has been slowly and steadily on the rise, the need for organs still far exceeds the number of organs donated. (For the latest statistics and more information, visit www.donatelifecalifornia.org.)

Religious Views and Concerns

Most major religions support organ donation. Reverence for life is the basis for almost all religious traditions, and organ donation is viewed as a life-saving act of compassion and generosity. Donated organs must be removed immediately after death, however, and some religions strongly believe that a deceased person's body should remain undisturbed, at least for a number of days. If you are uncertain about the right choice for you, it may be helpful to discuss the issue with your religious or spiritual adviser.

For a brief statement of different religions' views on organ donation, you can visit www.transweb.org; click on "FAQ."

Costs of Organ Donation

It will not cost your family anything if you want to donate your organs. The recipient pays the expenses, usually through insurance, Medicare, or Medicaid.

The Organ Donation Procedure

Before an organ is removed from a donor, two doctors who are not involved in the transplantation must declare that the patient is "irretrievably deceased" and brain-dead. Then the body is kept on a respirator to keep blood flowing though the organ until it can be removed and given to a waiting recipient. All of this usually takes about 24 hours.

Donation does not disfigure the body and does not interfere with having a funeral, even an open-casket service.

Specifying Your Wishes

Your advance directive is a good place to state your wishes regarding organ donation. Here's how to complete Part 3 of the form:

- Check box (a) if you want to donate any needed organs, tissues, or body parts.
- Check box (b) to specify the organs, tissues, or body parts that you are willing to donate. If you check this box, you must list the specific body parts—such as your corneas, heart, liver, kidneys, skin, or lungs—on the lines that follow the box.

Part (c) allows you to limit the purposes of your gift. If you don't want to place any restrictions on your gift, leave Part (c) as it is. But if you don't want your gift to be used for one or more of the listed purposes—transplant, therapy, research, or education—cross out any purposes you don't want.

If you do not wish to donate any organs, tissues, or body parts, you can leave this part of the form blank. You may also want to restrict your agent's power to authorize donation of your body parts, as shown in Part 1, Section (5), above.

FORM

Customizing your form. If you are making your advance directive using the downloadable form and you don't want to donate organs or other body parts after your death, you can delete Part 3 of the form. But if you do so, make sure to renumber the remaining parts and paragraph numbers so that everything stays in order.

Even if you use your advance directive to state that you wish to donate organs, there are a few other steps you can take to be sure your wishes are carried out. Start by registering with the state organ donor database at Donate Life California (donatelifecalifornia.org). It takes just a few minutes to sign up online. After your death, medical personnel will search the state donor registry and easily locate your wish to donate organs.

You can also indicate your wish to be an organ donor when you apply for a new California driver's license. If you do, a pink dot showing that you are a donor will be printed on your license. The DMV will also forward your information to Donate Life California, so if you use your driver's license to indicate that you want to donate, you don't have to separately register online.

Finally, and most importantly, you should discuss your views about organ donation with your health care agent, close relatives, and friends. Even if you've put your wishes in your advance directive and signed up with the donor registry, it's possible that an objection by a close relative could defeat your wishes after your death. The best thing you can do is let those close to you know that you feel strongly about donating your organs.

RESOURCE

More information. To learn more about organ donation, visit Donate Life California at www.donatelifecalifornia.org.

Part 4: Primary Physician

Here, if you like, you can enter the name and contact information of your primary physician (and an alternate primary physician) who you wish to oversee your medical care if possible. You will probably want to do this if you already have an established relationship with a doctor you trust and with whom you have discussed—or will discuss—your health care wishes. (For information about the importance of discussing your wishes with those who are likely to be involved with your care, see "Talking With Doctors," below.)

If you have more than one doctor and you're not sure which one to pick, think about who would do the best job of supervising your overall care. This may be your family doctor or general practitioner, rather than a specialist. If you're having trouble deciding, you may want to have conversations with each of them. After talking about your wishes, you may find that one of them seems more comfortable taking on the responsibility of managing your care, or that you have a better sense of whom you should pick. Remember, you can name one as your first choice and another as an alternate.

If you don't have an established relationship with a doctor, you'll do just as well to leave this part of your form blank and let your agent choose your health care providers if and when that becomes necessary.

 FORM

Customizing your form. If you are using the downloadable form to prepare your document and you don't want to name a primary physician, you can delete Part 4 from the form. Make sure you renumber the remaining parts and paragraphs accordingly.

Part 5: Making Your Advance Directive Legal

In this last part of your advance directive, you will finalize your document by signing it in front of either a notary public or two witnesses. (You don't have to do both.) If you are a resident in a nursing home, you must also comply with a special witnessing requirement. This section explains each alternative.

Notarization

A notary public is a licensed public officer who administers oaths and verifies signatures on documents. Finding a notary public shouldn't be a problem; many advertise online. A local bank, brokerage service, real estate office, or packaging store may also have onsite notaries. If you are a patient in a hospital, the hospital may provide notary services, or you can arrange for a notary to come to you. In most places, it won't cost more than $20 to have your signature notarized.

If you go to a notary, bring along some identification, such as your driver's license, that will prove that you are who you say you are. The notary will watch you sign your advance directive (in Section (13) of the document) and then sign it and stamp it with an official seal.

Witnesses

If you don't want to have your document notarized, you can sign it in front of two witnesses instead. Your witnesses must watch you sign your document and then sign the witness statements in Section (14).

Your witnesses must be adults, preferably ones who live nearby and will be readily available if it's ever necessary to prove that your advance directive is valid. In addition, neither witness can be:

- your health care agent
- your health care provider or an employee of your health care provider
- the operator or employee of a community care facility, such as a residential rehabilitation or counseling center, or
- the operator or employee of a residential care facility for the elderly.

Also, one of your witnesses must sign the witness statement in Section (15) declaring that the witness is not:

- related to you by blood, marriage, or adoption, or
- entitled to receive any part of your estate either under your will or by operation of law if you die without a will (usually, this means your close relatives).

Sample Advance Health Care Directive

Advance Health Care Directive

Explanation

You have the right to give instructions about your own health care. You also have the right to name someone else to make health care decisions for you. This form lets you do either or both of these things. It also lets you express your wishes regarding donation of organs and the designation of your primary physician. If you use this form, you may complete or modify all or any parts of it. You are free to use a different form.

Part 1 of this form is a power of attorney for health care. Part 1 lets you name another individual as agent to make health care decisions for you if you become incapable of making your own decisions or if you want someone else to make those decisions for you now even though you are still capable. You may also name an alternate agent to act for you if your first choice is not willing, able, or reasonably available to make decisions for you. (Your agent may not be an operator or employee of a community care facility or a residential care facility where you are receiving care, or your supervising health care provider or employee of the health care institution where you are receiving care, unless your agent is related to you, is your registered domestic partner, or is a coworker.)

Unless the form you sign limits the authority of your agent, your agent may make all health care decisions for you. This form has a place for you to limit the authority of your agent. You need not limit the authority of your agent if you wish to rely on your agent for all health care decisions that may have to be made. If you choose not to limit the authority of your agent, your agent will have the right to:

- Consent or refuse consent to any care, treatment, service, or procedure to maintain, diagnose, or otherwise affect a physical or mental condition.

- Select or discharge health care providers and institutions.
- Approve or disapprove diagnostic tests, surgical procedures, and programs of medication.
- Direct the provision, withholding, or withdrawal of artificial nutrition and hydration and all other forms of health care, including cardiopulmonary resuscitation.
- Make anatomical gifts, authorize an autopsy, and direct disposition of remains.

Part 2 of this form lets you give specific instructions about any aspect of your health care, whether or not you appoint an agent. Choices are provided for you to express your wishes regarding the provision, withholding, or withdrawal of treatment to keep you alive, as well as the provision of pain relief. Space is also provided for you to add to the choices you have made or for you to write out any additional wishes. If you are satisfied to allow your agent to determine what is best for you in making end-of-life decisions, you need not fill out Part 2 of this form.

Part 3 of this form lets you express an intention to donate your bodily organs and tissues following your death. Part 4 of this form lets you designate a physician to have primary responsibility for your health care.

After completing this form, sign and date the form at the end. The form must be signed by two qualified witnesses or acknowledged before a notary public. Give a copy of the signed and completed form to your physician, to any other health care providers you may have, to any health care institution at which you are receiving care, and to any health care agents you have named. You should talk to the person you have named as agent to make sure that he or she understands your wishes and is willing to take the responsibility. You have the right to revoke this advance health care directive or replace this form at any time.

Sample Advance Health Care Directive (continued)

Part 1: Power of Attorney for Health Care

1. **Designation of Agent:** I, _____Chester Larkin_____, of

   _16 Deerwood Drive, San Francisco_____,

   California, designate the following individual as my agent to make health care decisions for me:

   _Arthur Stimple_____
   Name of Individual You Choose as Agent

   _16 Deerwood Drive_____
   Address

San Francisco	_CA_	_94114_
City	State	Zip Code
_415-444-5555_	_415-444-1234_	
Home Phone	Work Phone	

   First Alternate Agent (Optional): If I revoke my agent's authority or if my agent is not willing, able, or reasonably available to make a health care decision for me, I designate as my first alternate agent:

   _Karen Larkin_____
   Name of Individual You Choose as First Alternate Agent

   _3421 Euclid Avenue_____
   Address

Berkeley	_CA_	_94709_
City	State	Zip Code
_510-555-5588_	_415-555-4000_	
Home Phone	Work Phone	

   Second Alternate Agent (Optional): If I revoke the authority of my agent and first alternate agent or if neither is willing, able, or reasonably available to make a health care decision for me, I designate as my second alternate agent:

   _____
   Name of Individual You Choose as Second Alternate Agent

   _____
   Address

City	State	Zip Code
Home Phone	Work Phone	

2. **Agent's Authority:** My agent is authorized to make all health care decisions for me, including decisions to provide, withhold, or withdraw artificial nutrition and hydration and all other forms of health care to keep me alive, except as I state here:

   _____

   _____

   _____

   _____

   _____

   Add additional sheets if needed

Sample Advance Health Care Directive (continued)

3. **When Agent's Authority Becomes Effective:** My agent's authority becomes effective when my primary physician determines that I am unable to make my own health care decisions unless I mark the following box. If I mark this box ☐ , my agent's authority to make health care decisions for me takes effect immediately.

4. **Agent's Obligation:** My agent shall make health care decisions for me in accordance with this power of attorney for health care, any instructions I give in Part 2 of this form, and my other wishes to the extent known to my agent. To the extent my wishes are unknown, my agent shall make health care decisions for me in accordance with what my agent determines to be in my best interest. In determining my best interest, my agent shall consider my personal values to the extent known to my agent.

5. **Agent's Postdeath Authority:** My agent is authorized to make anatomical gifts, authorize an autopsy, and direct disposition of my remains, except as I state here or in Part 3 of this form:

    I want my body to be cremated and my ashes to be scattered off the Marin Headlands.

    _____

    _____

    _____

    _____

    _____

    _____

    _____

    _____

    Add additional sheets if needed

6. **Nomination of Conservator:** If a conservator of my person needs to be appointed for me by a court, I nominate the agent designated in this form. If that agent is not willing, able, or reasonably available to act as conservator, I nominate the alternate agents whom I have named, in the order designated.

Part 2: Instructions for Health Care

(If you fill out this part of the form, you may strike any wording you do not want.)

7. **End-of-Life Decisions:** I direct that my health care providers and others involved in my care provide, withhold, or withdraw treatment in accordance with the choice I have marked below:

    ☒ **a. Choice Not to Prolong Life**

    I do not want my life to be prolonged if (1) I have an incurable and irreversible condition that will result in my death within a relatively short time, (2) I become unconscious and, to a reasonable degree of medical certainty, I will not regain consciousness, or (3) the likely risks and burdens of treatment would outweigh the expected benefits.

Sample Advance Health Care Directive (continued)

☐ ~~b. Choice to Prolong Life~~
~~I want my life to be prolonged as long as possible within the limits of generally accepted health care standards.~~

8. **Relief From Pain:** Except as I state in the following space, I direct that treatment for alleviation of pain or discomfort be provided at all times, even if it hastens my death:

_____

_____

_____

_____

_____

_____

_____

Add additional sheets if needed

9. **Other Wishes:** (*If you do not agree with any of the optional choices above and wish to write your own, or if you wish to add to the instructions you have given above, you may do so here.*) I direct that:

 I do not wish to receive artificial nutrition and hydration under

 any circumstances except for the treatment of a temporary

 condition in which I am unable to eat or drink, and then only

 for a short time. If, within a short time (as determined by my

 agent after consulting my doctor) there is no benefit to me, then

 I instruct that artificial nutrition and hydration be withdrawn.

_____

Add additional sheets if needed

Part 3: Donation of Organs at Death

10. **Wishes for Organ Donation:** Upon my death (*mark applicable box*):

 ☒ a. **I give any needed organs, tissues, or parts.**

 ☐ b. **I give the following organs, tissues, or parts only:**

_____

_____

_____

_____

_____

_____

Add additional sheets if needed

Sample Advance Health Care Directive (continued)

☐ **(c) My gift is for the following purposes** (*strike any of the following you do not want*):

1. Transplant

2. Therapy

3. Research

4. Education

Part 4: Primary Physician

11. **Designation of Primary Physician:** I designate the following physician as my primary physician:

Dr. Marcia Silverstein
_____
Name of Physician

555 9th Avenue
_____
Address

San Francisco   CA   94118
_____
City   State   Zip Code

415-261-2601
_____
Phone

Secondary Designation: If the physician I have designated above is not willing, able, or reasonably available to act as my primary physician, I designate the following physician as my primary physician:

_____
Name of Physician

_____
Address

_____
City   State   Zip Code

_____
Phone

Part 5: Signatures

12. **Effect of Copy:** A copy of this form has the same effect as the original.

13. **Signature:** (*Sign and date the form here.*)

Dated: _December 3, 20xx_____

Chester Larkin
_____
Your Signature

Chester Larkin
_____
Print Your Name

Sample Advance Health Care Directive (continued)

Alternative #1: Witnesses

14. **Statement of Witnesses:** I declare under penalty of perjury under the laws of California (1) that the individual who signed or acknowledged this advance health care directive is personally known to me, or that the individual's identity was proven to me by convincing evidence, (2) that the individual signed or acknowledged this advance directive in my presence, (3) that the individual appears to be of sound mind and under no duress, fraud, or undue influence, (4) that I am not a person appointed as agent by this advance directive, and (5) that I am not the individual's health care provider, an employee of the individual's health care provider, the operator of a community care facility, an employee of an operator of a community care facility, the operator of a residential care facility for the elderly, nor an employee of an operator of a residential care facility for the elderly.

First Witness

Chloe Abrams
Signature of Witness

Chloe Abrams
Print Name

2970 16th Street, San Francisco, CA 94103
Address

December 3, 20xx
Date

Second Witness

James Lee
Signature of Witness

James Lee
Print Name

849 Valencia Street, San Francisco, CA 94110
Address

December 3, 20xx
Date

15. **Additional Statement of Witnesses:** (*One of the above witnesses must also sign the following declaration.*)

I further declare under penalty of perjury under the laws of California that I am not related to the individual executing this advance health care directive by blood, marriage, or adoption, and to the best of my knowledge, I am not entitled to any part of the individual's estate upon his or her death under a will now existing or by operation of law.

James Lee
Signature of Witness

Sample Advance Health Care Directive (continued)

Alternative #2: Notarization

Certificate of Acknowledgment of Notary Public

> A notary public or other officer completing this certificate verifies only the identity of the individual who signed the document to which this certificate is attached, and not the truthfulness, accuracy, or validity of that document.

State of California

County of _____ } ss

On _____ , _____ , before me, _____ ,

personally appeared _____ , who

proved to me on the basis of satisfactory evidence to be the person(s) whose name(s) is/are subscribed to the within instrument and acknowledged to me that he/she/they executed the same in his/her/their authorized capacity(ies), and that by his/her/their signature(s) on the instrument the person(s), or the entity upon behalf of which the person(s) acted, executed the instrument.

I certify under PENALTY OF PERJURY under the laws of the State of California that the foregoing paragraph is true and correct.

WITNESS my hand and official seal.

_____

Notary Public for the State of California

[NOTARY SEAL]   My commission expires _____

16. **SPECIAL WITNESS REQUIREMENT:** (*The following statement is required only if you are a patient in a skilled nursing facility—a health care facility that provides skilled nursing care and supportive care to patients whose primary need is for availability of skilled nursing care on an extended basis. The patient advocate or ombudsman must sign the following statement.*)

Statement of Patient Advocate or Ombudsman

I declare under penalty of perjury under the laws of California that I am a patient advocate or ombudsman as designated by the State Department of Aging and that I am serving as a witness as required by Section 4675 of the Probate Code.

_____

Signature of Patient Advocate or Ombudsman

_____

Print Name

_____

Address

_____

Date

It's not usually difficult to satisfy this last requirement. You can ask a neighbor or friend to witness your document, so long as you're not leaving that person anything in your will.

Patients in Skilled Nursing Facilities

If, at the time you sign your document, you are a patient in a nursing home or another health care facility that provides long-term nursing and supportive care, you must obtain the signature of the facility's patient advocate or ombudsman in Paragraph (16) of your form. This requirement applies whether you have your document notarized or witnessed, as described just above.

 FORM

Customizing your form. If you are making your advance directive using the downloadable form, you can delete whichever options you do not use to finalize your document. In other words, you can get rid of the unused notary or witness statements. Remember to renumber any paragraphs remaining at the end of your form, if necessary.

What to Do After You Complete Your Advance Directive

By taking the time and making the effort to draw up your advance directive, you have already done much to ensure that your wishes will be followed. The next step is to make your wishes for your future health care widely known.

Distributing Copies

Some people are hesitant to discuss the particulars of their medical care with other people, feeling that it is an intensely private issue. However, in the case of health care documents, you must weigh your desire for privacy against the need for the documents to

be effective. Your carefully prepared medical directive will be wasted unless you make sure it gets into the hands of the people who need to know about it.

Registering Your Advance Directive

For a $10 fee, you can register basic information about your advance directive in a database maintained by the California Secretary of State. The form you file states that you've made an advance directive, provides the name of your health care agent, and says where you keep the document, so that others can find it. You don't have to disclose the details of your health care wishes when you register. Registry information is available on request to health care providers. Currently, doctors and hospitals rarely use the registry system to find out whether a patient has an advance directive, but it's not very expensive to register and it certainly can't hurt you. If health care providers begin to use the registry more frequently, it may turn out to be helpful.

The form you need to register your advance directive is available through the Secretary of State's website at www.sos.ca.gov/registries. (Select "Advance Health Care Directive Registry" to get started.) Or, you can call the Secretary of State's office for more information at 916-653-3984.

At a minimum, give copies of your signed and completed advance directive to the doctors or medical facility most likely to be treating you and to your health care agent. Also think about giving copies to immediate family members and friends. Here's a complete list of people and institutions to whom you may want to give copies:

- any physician you consult regularly
- the agent you named in your directive
- the office of the hospital or other care facility in which you are likely to receive treatment

- the patient representative of your HMO or insurance plan (you can call your plan's business office to find out who this person is and how to make contact)
- close relatives, particularly immediate family members—spouse, children, siblings, and
- trusted friends.

A copy of your advance directive is every bit as legally valid as the original. (Your form clearly states this in Section (12).)

Talking With Doctors

There is no substitute for discussing your medical preferences with the doctors who will be likely to provide your care. If you do have a regular doctor, or if you are approaching major surgery or some other serious medical event and have been assigned to a specialist, talk over your medical directives with him or her. If you have other concerns about your medical condition, such as the effects of certain treatments or the probability of carrying on certain life activities, discuss those, too.

Talking With Family Members and Friends

It is also wise to discuss your health care directives and other medical care concerns with the people who are likely to oversee or witness your care. Those who make the effort to discuss these issues usually find it worthwhile. Not only do those involved get peace of mind in knowing true wishes, the knowledge can often be a bridge to closer relationships. If the topic seems too difficult to broach, consider using a relevant book, magazine article, television show, or film as a catalyst for discussion.

Preparing a Wallet Card

If you are involved in a serious accident or another medical emergency, a wallet card like the one below can alert emergency medical personnel to the existence of your advance directive. You may want to complete one of these cards to carry with you—keep it in a conspicuous place in your wallet—and give another card to your spouse, agent, or another person who is likely to be contacted in an emergency. Remember to make new cards if any of the information on the card changes.

You can find a tear-out wallet card in Appendix B or you can download a card from Nolo's website (see Appendix A for the link).

Attention: Emergency Medical Personnel

I, _____ ,
[insert your name] of _____
_____ [insert your address]
have prepared an advance health care directive stating the type of medical care I wish to receive if I am incapacitated and unable to speak for myself. I have also appointed a health care agent to oversee my wishes. In the event of a medical emergency, please contact one of the people listed on the reverse of this card, in the order listed.

©Nolo 2016   [OVER]

My Agent: _____
_____ [insert agent's name and phone numbers where agent can be reached in an emergency]

My Alternate Agent:_____
_____

My Primary Physician: _____
_____

[insert your doctor's name and phone number]

My advance health care directive is located: _____
_____

[insert the location of an easy-to-find copy of your directive]

Keeping Your Documents Up to Date

It's a good idea to review your health care documents occasionally—at least once a year—to make sure they still accurately reflect your wishes. Advances in technology and changes in your health are two shifts in course that may prompt you to change your mind about the kind of health care you want.

In addition, you should consider making new documents if:

You move to another state. Most states have laws honoring advance directives that are properly prepared under the laws of another state. Nevertheless, if you move, it's a good idea to prepare a new advance directive using your new state's official form. Health care providers in your new state will be most familiar with that state's form, and this will most likely make it easier for your agent to manage your care.

You made and finalized a health care directive many years ago. An advance directive made under an old law is valid, but it's wise to keep your document up to date. Health care providers and hospitals will be most comfortable honoring the state's most recent advance directive form. Even if the state laws have not changed since you made your advance directive, those who must rely on your document will feel most confident doing so if the form was made within the past five years; that way, it leaves little room for doubt that the form reflects your current wishes for care.

The agent you named to supervise your wishes becomes unable to do so. If your first choice as agent becomes unavailable before your document has taken effect, you may want to make a new directive to name a new agent. It's true that if you appoint an alternate agent, that person will take the job if it's ever necessary. But if you already know your agent is unavailable, it's smart to name someone new—perhaps just moving your alternate into the first position and naming another alternate to back up that person. This helps to ensure someone will always be available to make decisions for you.

If you make new advance directive, you should formally revoke your old one. (See below.)

You get divorced. If you named your spouse or registered domestic partner as your health care agent, it's wise to make a new directive to name a new agent. (See "When Your Advance Directive Ends," above.)

Revoking an Advance Directive

You can revoke your advance directive at any time, as long as you are of sound mind. California law presumes that you have the capacity to revoke your documents whenever you wish, so anyone who challenges your ability to revoke a document bears the burden of proving that you are no longer of sound mind. (Cal. Prob. Code § 4657.)

If you want to cancel your advance directive for any reason, it's best to do so in writing. Giving a written Notice of Revocation to your health care agent and anyone else who has a copy of your advance directive eliminates confusion and helps to ensure that your most recent wishes will be honored. We provide a simple revocation form that you can use, both as a download from Nolo's website and as a tear-out form in Appendix B. (See Appendix A for a link to the downloadable form.) A sample is shown below.

In addition to preparing the Notice of Revocation, you should tear up the original document and all copies. Make sure that all people who have copies of your advance directive return them to you to be destroyed.

If you have a change of heart about your health care wishes but are unable to prepare a Notice of Revocation, you can tell any health care provider—for example, a doctor or nurse when you're in the hospital—that you want to cancel your advance directive. The health care provider is required to promptly communicate

Revocation of Advance Health Care Directive

I, ___Faith Douglass_____ ,

of the City of ___Bakersfield_____ , County of ___Kern_____ ,

State of California, revoke the advance health care directive dated ___July 12, 20xx_____ ,

empowering ___Tyler Douglass_____

to make health care decisions for me. I revoke and withdraw all power and authority granted under that

directive.

Dated: ___May 3, 20xx_____

___*Faith Douglass*_____
Signature of Principal

___Faith Douglass_____
Print Principal's Name

your wishes to your supervising health care provider (your primary doctor) and to any health care institution where you are receiving care. (Cal. Prob. Code § 4696.) The supervising health care provider must then act quickly to note the revocation in your medical record. (Cal. Prob. Code § 4731(a).)

If, however, you wish to revoke the authority of your health care agent—not just change your health care wishes—and you are unable to do so in writing, you must communicate this directly to the doctor who is supervising your care at the time you want to revoke your document. (Cal. Prob. Code § 4695(a).)

How to Revoke an Advance Health Care Directive

☐ Prepare and sign a Notice of Revocation. (Unlike the advance directive itself, your signature doesn't need to be notarized or witnessed.)

☐ Deliver a copy of the Notice of Revocation to your health care agent and anyone else who has a copy of your advance directive.

☐ Destroy your original, signed advance directive.

☐ Obtain all copies of your advance directive and destroy them, too.

Do Not Resuscitate (DNR) and POLST Forms

How DNR Forms Work.. 52

Preparing a DNR Form... 52

What to Do After You Complete a DNR Form.. 54

Revoking a DNR Form 54

About POLST Forms.. 54

In addition to an advance directive, there are two other forms you can use to specify your wishes for end-of-life medical treatment. The first is called a Prehospital Do Not Resuscitate Form, or DNR form. The second is a newer form known as POLST, which stands for "Physician Orders for Life-Sustaining Treatment." These forms typically come into play late in life, when someone is very close to death from a progressive illness or old age. A patient may have one form or the other; it is usually not necessary to have both. DNR forms and POLSTs must be reviewed and signed by a doctor.

A DNR form directs emergency medical personnel not to administer cardiopulmonary resuscitation (CPR) in the event of a medical emergency. It's called a "prehospital" DNR form because it covers emergencies that occur when you are not in the hospital—for example, if you collapse at home. If you are hospitalized, doctors can add a DNR form to your medical record if you wish.

A POLST is similar to a DNR form, but it covers more types of treatment. POLST forms are used in hospitals, nursing homes, and hospice care settings; they travel with patients from place to place, remaining part of the medical record. A POLST sets out your wishes about CPR and other critical, life-sustaining treatments at the end of life, though it is not a substitute for an advance directive.

This chapter discusses DNR and POLST forms in more detail, showing samples of each.

How DNR Forms Work

Emergency response teams must act quickly in a medical crisis. They do not have the time to determine whether you have a valid advance directive explaining treatments you want provided or withheld. Even if you carry a wallet card alerting emergency medical personnel to the existence of your advance directive (see Chapter 2), they probably won't be able to obtain the document right away. If they do not know your wishes, they must provide you with all possible life-saving measures. This means that it may be wise to consider a DNR form if you:

- have a terminal illness and know you would not want to be given CPR
- have a high risk for cardiac or respiratory arrest, or
- have strong feelings against the use of CPR under any circumstances.

You can make sure that emergency care providers know about your DNR form by wearing an easily identifiable bracelet, anklet, or necklace. (Instructions for ordering one are below.) If emergency personnel know of the DNR form, they will not administer CPR.

If you ask to have CPR withheld, you will not be provided with:

- chest compression
- electric shock treatments to the chest
- tubes placed in the airway to assist breathing
- artificial ventilation, or
- cardiac drugs.

Preparing a DNR Form

This chapter shows a sample of the official DNR form available from the California Emergency Medical Services Authority. You can download the form for free from the EMSA website at http://www.emsa.ca.gov/DNR_and_POLST_Forms or call 916-322-4336 and ask to have a form mailed to you.

A DNR form is easy to prepare. Fill in your name and sign the form; then have your doctor do the same. (Your doctor must sign the DNR form to make it legally valid. (Cal. Prob. Code § 4780).) The form comes with easy instructions that tell you what to do.

Sample Prehospital Do Not Resuscitate (DNR) Form

EMERGENCY MEDICAL SERVICES
PREHOSPITAL DO NOT RESUSCITATE (DNR) FORM

An Advance Request to Limit the Scope of Emergency Medical Care

I, _____ , request limited emergency care as herein described.
(print patient's name)

I understand DNR means that if my heart stops beating or if I stop breathing, no medical procedure to restart breathing or heart functioning will be instituted.

I understand this decision will not prevent me from obtaining other emergency medical care by prehospital emergency medical care personnel and/or medical care directed by a physician prior to my death.

I understand that I may revoke this directive at any time by destroying this form and removing any "DNR" medallions.

I give permission for this information to be given to the prehospital emergency care personnel, doctors, nurses or other health personnel as necessary to implement this directive.

I hereby agree to the "Do Not Resuscitate" (DNR) order.

_____   _____
Patient/Surrogate Signature   Date

_____
Surrogate's Relationship to Patient

By signing this form, the surrogate acknowledges that this request to forgo resuscitative measures is consistent with the known desires of, and with the best interest of, the individual who is the subject of this form.

I affirm that this patient/surrogate is making an informed decision and that this directive is the expressed wish of the patient/surrogate. A copy of this form is in the patient's permanent medical record.

In the event of cardiac or respiratory arrest, no chest compressions, assisted ventilations, intubation, defibrillation, or cardiotonic medications are to be initiated.

_____   _____
Physician Signature   Date

_____   _____
Print Name   Telephone

THIS FORM WILL NOT BE ACCEPTED IF IT HAS BEEN AMENDED OR ALTERED IN ANY WAY

PREHOSPITAL DNR REQUEST FORM

Copy 1 – To be kept by patient

What to Do After You Complete a DNR Form

Wearing a DNR necklace or bracelet is the best way to tell emergency medical personnel that you do not wish to be resuscitated. You can obtain a bracelet or medallion from the MedicAlert Foundation; visit www.medicalert.org or call 800-432-5378. You will need to submit a copy of the signed DNR order with your MedicAlert application.

You must pay an annual membership fee to join MedicAlert, plus the cost of the DNR bracelet or medallion. Prices for medallions start at around $30, though you can pay hundreds of dollars for a designer version made of precious metals.

If you prepare a DNR form, discuss your decision with your family or other caretakers. Tell them where your form is located and who you want them to alert if you require emergency treatment. For example, in addition to calling 911, you may want someone to alert your primary physician that you're in trouble. Even if you are wearing identification, such as a bracelet or necklace, keep the form in an obvious place. You might consider keeping it by your bedside, on the front of your refrigerator, in your wallet, or in your suitcase if you are traveling. If your DNR form is not apparent and immediately available, or if it has been altered in any way, CPR will most likely be performed.

You may also wish to give a copy of the DNR form to your physician, so that it can be made part of your medical record.

Revoking a DNR Form

If you change your mind and want to revoke your DNR form, you should destroy the DNR form and any copies, and make sure everyone you've told about your DNR form knows that you have revoked it. There is no revocation form to fill out.

And, obviously, you should remove any DNR medallions that you have been wearing.

 RESOURCE

More information about DNR forms. To find out more about DNR forms, call the California Medical Association at 800-786-4262.

About POLST Forms

A Physician Orders for Life-Sustaining Treatment (POLST) form is a doctor's order that helps you keep control over medical care at the end of life. Like a DNR form, a POLST tells emergency medical personnel and other health care providers whether or not to administer cardiopulmonary resuscitation (CPR) in the event of a medical emergency. It may be used in addition to—or instead of—a DNR form.

Unlike a DNR form, a POLST also includes directions about life-sustaining measures in addition to CPR, such as intubation, antibiotic use, and feeding tubes. The POLST helps medical providers understand your wishes at a glance, but it is *not* a substitute for a properly prepared advance directive.

An advance directive provides more information than a POLST form does, including details about your health care agent, more complete health care wishes, and your preference for organ donation. So if you have a POLST, you do not need a DNR form, but you should still complete an advance directive to provide a full set of wishes about your care.

To be legally valid, a POLST form must be signed by:

- a physician, nurse practitioner, or physician assistant acting under the supervision of the physician and within the scope of practice authorized by law, and
- you or your legally recognized health care decisionmaker. (Cal. Prob. Code § 4780.)

Physician Orders for Life-Sustaining Treatment (POLST) Form

HIPAA PERMITS DISCLOSURE OF POLST TO OTHER HEALTH CARE PROVIDERS AS NECESSARY

Physician Orders for Life-Sustaining Treatment (POLST)

EMSA #111 B
(Effective 1/1/2016)*

First follow these orders, then contact Physician/NP/PA. A copy of the signed POLST form is a legally valid physician order. Any section not completed implies full treatment for that section. **POLST complements an Advance Directive and is not intended to replace that document.**

Patient Last Name:	Date Form Prepared:
Patient First Name:	Patient Date of Birth:
Patient Middle Name:	Medical Record #: *(optional)*

A Check One	**CARDIOPULMONARY RESUSCITATION (CPR):** *If patient has no pulse and is not breathing.* *If patient is NOT in cardiopulmonary arrest, follow orders in Sections B and C.*
	☐ **Attempt Resuscitation/CPR** (Selecting CPR in Section A **requires** selecting Full Treatment in Section B)
	☐ **Do Not Attempt Resuscitation/DNR** (Allow Natural Death)

B Check One	**MEDICAL INTERVENTIONS:** *If patient is found with a pulse and/or is breathing.*
	☐ **Full Treatment – primary goal of prolonging life by all medically effective means.** In addition to treatment described in Selective Treatment and Comfort-Focused Treatment, use intubation, advanced airway interventions, mechanical ventilation, and cardioversion as indicated.
	☐ *Trial Period of Full Treatment.*
	☐ **Selective Treatment** – **goal of treating medical conditions while avoiding burdensome measures.** In addition to treatment described in Comfort-Focused Treatment, use medical treatment, IV antibiotics, and IV fluids as indicated. Do not intubate. May use non-invasive positive airway pressure. Generally avoid intensive care.
	☐ *Request transfer to hospital only if comfort needs cannot be met in current location.*
	☐ **Comfort-Focused Treatment** – **primary goal of maximizing comfort.** Relieve pain and suffering with medication by any route as needed; use oxygen, suctioning, and manual treatment of airway obstruction. Do not use treatments listed in Full and Selective Treatment unless consistent with comfort goal. *Request transfer to hospital only if comfort needs cannot be met in current location.*
	Additional Orders: _____

C Check One	**ARTIFICIALLY ADMINISTERED NUTRITION:** *Offer food by mouth if feasible and desired.*
	☐ Long-term artificial nutrition, including feeding tubes. Additional Orders: _____
	☐ Trial period of artificial nutrition, including feeding tubes. _____
	☐ No artificial means of nutrition, including feeding tubes. _____

D	**INFORMATION AND SIGNATURES:**

Discussed with: ☐ Patient (Patient Has Capacity)   ☐ Legally Recognized Decisionmaker

☐ Advance Directive dated _____, available and reviewed →	Health Care Agent if named in Advance Directive:
☐ Advance Directive not available	Name: _____
☐ No Advance Directive	Phone: _____

Signature of Physician / Nurse Practitioner / Physician Assistant (Physician/NP/PA)
My signature below indicates to the best of my knowledge that these orders are consistent with the patient's medical condition and preferences.

Print Physician/NP/PA Name:	Physician/NP/PA Phone #:	Physician/PA License #, NP Cert. #:
Physician/NP/PA Signature: *(required)*		Date:

Signature of Patient or Legally Recognized Decisionmaker
I am aware that this form is voluntary. By signing this form, the legally recognized decisionmaker acknowledges that this request regarding resuscitative measures is consistent with the known desires of, and with the best interest of, the individual who is the subject of the form.

Print Name:	Relationship: *(write self if patient)*
Signature: *(required)*	Date:	**FOR REGISTRY USE ONLY**
Mailing Address (street/city/state/zip):	Phone Number:	

SEND FORM WITH PATIENT WHENEVER TRANSFERRED OR DISCHARGED

*Form versions with effective dates of 1/1/2009, 4/1/2011 or 10/1/2014 are also valid

Physician Orders for Life-Sustaining Treatment (POLST) Form, page 2

HIPAA PERMITS DISCLOSURE OF POLST TO OTHER HEALTH CARE PROVIDERS AS NECESSARY

Patient Information

Name (last, first, middle):		Date of Birth:	Gender: **M F**
NP/PA's Supervising Physician Name:		**Preparer Name** (if other than signing Physician/NP/PA) Name/Title:	Phone #:

Additional Contact   □ None

Name:	Relationship to Patient:	Phone #:

Directions for Health Care Provider

Completing POLST

- **Completing a POLST form is voluntary.** California law requires that a POLST form be followed by healthcare providers, and provides immunity to those who comply in good faith. In the hospital setting, a patient will be assessed by a physician, or a nurse practitioner (NP) or a physician assistant (PA) acting under the supervision of the physician, who will issue appropriate orders that are consistent with the patient's preferences.
- **POLST does not replace the Advance Directive.** When available, review the Advance Directive and POLST form to ensure consistency, and update forms appropriately to resolve any conflicts.
- POLST must be completed by a health care provider based on patient preferences and medical indications.
- A legally recognized decisionmaker may include a court-appointed conservator or guardian, agent designated in an Advance Directive, orally designated surrogate, spouse, registered domestic partner, parent of a minor, closest available relative, or person whom the patient's physician/NP/PA believes best knows what is in the patient's best interest and will make decisions in accordance with the patient's expressed wishes and values to the extent known.
- A legally recognized decisionmaker may execute the POLST form only if the patient lacks capacity or has designated that the decisionmaker's authority is effective immediately.
- To be valid a POLST form must be signed by (1) a physician, or by a nurse practitioner or a physician assistant acting under the supervision of a physician and within the scope of practice authorized by law and (2) the patient or decisionmaker. Verbal orders are acceptable with follow-up signature by physician/NP/PA in accordance with facility/community policy.
- If a translated form is used with patient or decisionmaker, attach it to the signed English POLST form.
- Use of original form is strongly encouraged. Photocopies and FAXes of signed POLST forms are legal and valid. A copy should be retained in patient's medical record, on Ultra Pink paper when possible.

Using POLST

- Any incomplete section of POLST implies full treatment for that section.

Section A:

- If found pulseless and not breathing, no defibrillator (including automated external defibrillators) or chest compressions should be used on a patient who has chosen "Do Not Attempt Resuscitation."

Section B:

- When comfort cannot be achieved in the current setting, the patient, including someone with "Comfort-Focused Treatment," should be transferred to a setting able to provide comfort (e.g., treatment of a hip fracture).
- Non-invasive positive airway pressure includes continuous positive airway pressure (CPAP), bi-level positive airway pressure (BiPAP), and bag valve mask (BVM) assisted respirations.
- IV antibiotics and hydration generally are not "Comfort-Focused Treatment."
- Treatment of dehydration prolongs life. If a patient desires IV fluids, indicate "Selective Treatment" or "Full Treatment."
- Depending on local EMS protocol, "Additional Orders" written in Section B may not be implemented by EMS personnel.

Reviewing POLST

It is recommended that POLST be reviewed periodically. Review is recommended when:

- The patient is transferred from one care setting or care level to another, or
- There is a substantial change in the patient's health status, or
- The patient's treatment preferences change.

Modifying and Voiding POLST

- A patient with capacity can, at any time, request alternative treatment or revoke a POLST by any means that indicates intent to revoke. It is recommended that revocation be documented by drawing a line through Sections A through D, writing "VOID" in large letters, and signing and dating this line.
- A legally recognized decisionmaker may request to modify the orders, in collaboration with the physician/NP/PA, based on the known desires of the patient or, if unknown, the patient's best interests.

This form is approved by the California Emergency Medical Services Authority in cooperation with the statewide POLST Task Force. For more information or a copy of the form, visit **www.caPOLST.org**.

SEND FORM WITH PATIENT WHENEVER TRANSFERRED OR DISCHARGED

When you enter a medical facility or another health care setting, such as home hospice with professional nursing care, a health care professional will prepare the POLST with your guidance, or with help from your health care agent. (If you did not appoint a health care agent, doctors will turn to your close family members for direction.) If a medical staff person does not ask you whether you want to create a POLST, you may request one. In California, a POLST form is usually printed on bright pink paper so it will stand out in your medical records.

For your reference, this chapter shows a sample POLST form. You can learn more about POLSTs by visiting www.capolst.org.

Durable Powers of Attorney for Finances

How Durable Powers of Attorney for Finances Work..60

    Who Can Make a Durable Power of Attorney for Finances..60

    When Your Document Becomes Effective..60

    When the Power of Attorney Ends...63

    How Much It Costs...68

    Will Your Power of Attorney Be Accepted?...69

About Your Agent for Finances...70

    Powers You Can Grant...70

    What Your Agent Can't Do..70

    Legal Responsibilities...71

    Choosing Your Agent...74

    Paying Your Agent..78

Preparing Your Durable Power of Attorney...79

    Getting Started...79

    Your Name and Address...79

    Naming Your Agent...80

    Granting Powers to Your Agent...80

    Adding Special Instructions...86

    If You Appointed More Than One Agent..95

    Reliance by Third Parties..96

    Signing Your Durable Power of Attorney..96

    Agent's Acceptance of Responsibility...96

Making Your Durable Power of Attorney Legal...96

    Before You Sign...96

    Sign and Notarize the Durable Power of Attorney...96

    Putting Your Durable Power of Attorney on Public Record...100

    What to Do With the Signed Document...100

    Making and Distributing Copies...101

    Keeping Your Document Up to Date..101

Revoking a Durable Power of Attorney for Finances...101

    When to Revoke a Durable Power of Attorney for Finances..101

    How to Revoke a Durable Power of Attorney for Finances..102

Making a durable power of attorney for finances ensures that someone you trust will have the legal authority to manage the many practical financial tasks that will arise if you become incapacitated—from paying bills to handling insurance, government benefits, and other matters. This chapter tells you what you need to know to understand and prepare your California durable power of attorney document.

How Durable Powers of Attorney for Finances Work

Before you jump into the process of making your durable power of attorney for finances, it's a good idea to know a little bit about how the document works in the real world. This section covers the following important issues:

- who can make a valid power of attorney
- how much it costs to make a power of attorney
- when a power of attorney becomes effective (either right away or only if you are incapacitated)
- how to make sure your power of attorney will be accepted by banks, government agencies, and others, and
- when a power of attorney ends.

Who Can Make a Durable Power of Attorney for Finances

You can create a valid power of attorney for finances if you are an adult (at least 18 years old) and of sound mind. For a more detailed discussion, see "The Mental Capacity Requirement" in Chapter 1.

When Your Document Becomes Effective

There are two kinds of durable powers of attorney for finances: those that take effect immediately and those that never take effect unless a doctor (or two, if you wish) declares that you can no longer manage your financial affairs. Which kind you should choose depends, in part, on when you want your agent to begin handling tasks for you.

You Want Someone to Take Over Now

If you want someone to take over some or all of your affairs now, you should make your document effective as soon as you sign it. (In California, your document is effective when you sign unless you specify otherwise.) Then, your agent can begin helping you with your financial tasks right away—and can continue to do so if you later become incapacitated.

You don't have to be incapacitated to benefit from a durable power of attorney. If you make your document effective immediately, your agent can step in right away to help you manage your financial affairs. This may make sense in a number of different situations, including when:

- you are suffering from a short- or long-term illness and you don't have the energy to deal with day-to-day financial tasks
- you have an injury that makes it difficult to get to your financial institutions to take care of important money matters, or
- you've been occasionally forgetful and feel that it would be safer to have someone else keep an eye on your finances.

Even if you give your agent permission to start handling your finances before you become incapacitated, you don't have to turn over complete control. Explain to your agent what you want done. Your agent should follow your wishes carefully. And if you want your agent to consult you before taking action under the power of attorney, he or she is legally obligated to do so. If you ever become dissatisfied with the arrangement, you can revoke the durable power and end the agent's authority to act for you.

You Want Your Agent to Take Over Only If You Become Incapacitated

On the other hand, you may feel strongly that your agent should not take over unless you are incapacitated. In this case, you have two options. If you trust your agent to act only when it's absolutely necessary, you can go ahead and make an immediately effective document. Legally, your agent will then have the authority to act on your behalf—but won't do so until he or she decides you cannot handle your affairs yourself.

If you're uncomfortable giving your agent authority now, you can add language to your durable power of attorney to make what's known as a "springing" document. It won't take effect until a physician examines you and declares, in writing, that you can't manage your finances.

There are some real inconveniences involved in creating a springing power of attorney, and it's wise to consider them before you decide to make one. If you truly trust your agent, you may find that it makes more sense to create a document that takes effect immediately and then make clear to your agent when to take action.

Making your document effective immediately. If you know, or reasonably believe, that you are likely to become incapacitated soon, it's probably a good idea to make your durable power of attorney effective right away. For example, this would be appropriate if you or someone you love has a serious degenerative disease and is rapidly losing the ability to manage business affairs. Or, if you are facing major surgery, you will probably want to sign an immediately effective document.

Even if you're 100% healthy now, if you're comfortable giving another person the authority to manage your affairs, and your agent is trustworthy (you shouldn't appoint anyone that you don't trust completely), you're probably better off making your document effective immediately. That avoids the hassles of creating a springing power of attorney, discussed in the following section. You can agree with your agent that no action will be taken under the document until, in the agent's opinion, you are unable to take care of your finances—or you otherwise direct your agent to take action. If you aren't confident that your agent will refrain from using the document for as long as you are able to handle your own affairs, think about naming someone else to represent you.

What Is Incapacity?

Incapacity is not a recognized medical condition. For purposes of your durable power of attorney for finances, incapacity means that you no longer have the ability to handle your own financial transactions, either because you can no longer communicate your wishes or because you cannot understand:

- the rights, duties, and responsibilities created or affected by your financial decisions
- the probable consequences of your financial decisions, or
- the significant risks, benefits, and reasonable alternatives involved in your financial decisions.

(These guidelines are set out in Section 812 of the California Probate Code and Section 39 of the California Civil Code.)

Common physical causes of incapacity are problems generally associated with advancing age, such as heart attacks, strokes, and Alzheimer's disease. Incapacity can also be caused by serious accidents, drug or alcohol addiction, or degenerative diseases such as AIDS or mental illness. People sometimes move in and out of periods of incapacity. (For information about what happens if you regain capacity and want to revoke your power of attorney, see "Revoking a Durable Power of Attorney for Finances" at the end of this chapter.)

If you choose to make your document effective immediately, you and your agent should discuss what "incapacity" means to you. You'll want a clear understanding of when your agent should step in. That moment may be when your agent sees that you're too ill to pay your bills on time or that you have lost the mental acuity to make responsible decisions about your investments. Explore various scenarios with your agent until you reach an understanding of when and how your agent should exercise authority under the document.

Making the power of attorney effective later. You may not want your agent to take over your financial affairs until a doctor states that you are no longer able to manage them on your own. If this is so, you can make a "springing" power of attorney. It has absolutely no effect unless and until at least one physician signs a sworn statement that you are incapacitated.

Some people prefer this kind of durable power of attorney because they're not in immediate danger of incapacity. The document simply acts as a kind of risk-free legal insurance—something to protect you if you ever need it.

Others may like the idea of a springing document because requiring at least one doctor's statement removes any danger that an agent will make a judgment that someone is incapacitated—even if that person disagrees. Ideally, however, you will trust your agent so well that this will not be a serious concern.

There are some real drawbacks to springing powers of attorney that you should consider.

First, for your document to spring into effect, your agent will have to obtain statements from one or two doctors (the number is up to you) certifying that you can no longer handle your financial affairs. To authorize your agent to get these statements, you must fill out a form permitting the doctors to release confidential health care information to your agent. This step is required by the Health Insurance Portability

and Accountability Act, or HIPAA. The form is officially titled "Authorization for Disclosure and Use of Protected Health Information," but we call it a "HIPAA release" for short. This book contains a HIPAA release you can fill out and give to your agent. (You can find a sample below. The blank form is in Appendix B and downloadable from Nolo's website; see Appendix A for the link. You'll see that the HIPAA form uses larger type than other forms. That's required by California law)

Why Must a Doctor Make the Decision?

Because incapacity isn't a distinct medical condition, it may seem unnecessary to have a physician make the determination that you can no longer handle your finances. But it's almost always done that way, even though California law doesn't expressly require it.

A doctor's statement is familiar and reassuring to the people your agent will have to deal with. Banks and other institutions would probably be unwilling to rely on a statement by a family member or close friend that you are unable to handle your affairs.

However, as discussed above, if you don't want to involve doctors in this decision, you can make an immediately effective document and let your agent decide when to start using the authority it grants.

Your agent will need to take the HIPAA release form to the doctors, and the doctors will need to examine you and perhaps order diagnostic tests. The process of getting the doctors' statements will undoubtedly be time-consuming and at least a little bit complicated.

In addition, some people may be reluctant to accept a springing power of attorney, even though your agent has obtained the required doctors' statements and your document is perfectly legal. A bank, for example, might question whether you have, in fact, become incapacitated. These hassles could delay your agent and disrupt the handling of your finances.

With a springing durable power of attorney, someone must be responsible for judging whether or not you are incapacitated. Otherwise, there's no way for the document to go into effect. When you make a durable power of attorney using this book, you have a couple of options. You can:

- name (in your power of attorney document) one or two doctors to make the determination, or
- allow your agent to choose one or two doctors if the need arises.

Along with the HIPAA release form, a form for the doctor to sign, called Physician's Determination of Incapacity, is included in this book. (You'll find a sample below, and blank forms in Appendix B downloadable from Nolo's website; see Appendix A for the link.) After the physician has signed a statement documenting your incapacity, the agent can attach it to the original power of attorney. Then, if anyone questions the agent's authority to act for you, the agent can produce the statement.

If you name the doctor yourself, be sure the person you've chosen is willing to make the incapacity determination for you. And be certain you and the doctor are in basic agreement about what "incapacitated" means to you. If you decide to let your agent choose the doctor, you should have a conversation about incapacity with your agent. He or she will need to discuss the issue with the doctor if the time comes.

If you name a specific doctor to certify your incapacity and that doctor is not available when a physician's statement is needed, your agent can choose another doctor to make the determination.

If no one objects to the doctor's statement that you are incapacitated, your document should take effect without any trouble. But if third parties raise a fuss (not likely, but it sometimes happens), a court may have to make the final decision about your ability to take care of yourself and your property.

One Doctor or Two?

If you're comfortable with the idea of naming one doctor to make this determination, there's no need to require a second physician's statement. If it worries you to leave the decision in the hands of just one person, take a moment to consider whether you're comfortable making this power of attorney document. Do you truly trust the person who will be your agent? Do you fear that family members will make trouble for your agent and try to interfere with your plans? If you are experiencing a lot of anxiety about making the document, talk with family members and the person who will be your agent to get a clearer idea of whether they support what you are doing. If you're still uncomfortable after you've tried to talk things out, you may want to consult a lawyer about legal means to assuage your fears.

When the Power of Attorney Ends

A durable power of attorney for finances is valid until you revoke it, you die, or there is no one to serve as your agent. Very infrequently, a court invalidates a power of attorney.

You revoke the power of attorney. As long as you are of sound mind, you can revoke a power of attorney for finances at any time, whether or not it has taken effect. All you need to do is fill out a simple revocation form, sign it in front of a notary public, and give copies to the agent and to people or institutions the agent has been dealing with. This book contains revocation forms for you to use. (Sample forms are shown at the end of this chapter; you can find blank forms in Appendix B and download them from Nolo's website; see Appendix A for the link.) Keep these forms on hand in case you need them later.

Sample HIPAA Release

Authorization for Disclosure and Use of Protected Health Information

Authorization. I, _____ Alice Murphy _____ , hereby authorize the disclosure and release of any of my individually identifiable health information and any other medical records ("my medical records") to the following person(s) who has or have been designated by me to act as my agent, attorney-in-fact, successor trustee, or other personal representative, hereafter referred to individually or collectively as "my agent."

Janine Radcliffe	2112 Palm Court, Orange, CA 92856	714-333-5544
Name of Agent	Address	Telephone

Trevor Murphy	55 Citrus Drive, Orange, CA 92856	714-222-3377
Name of Agent	Address	Telephone

Name of Agent	Address	Telephone

Purpose. This authorization is for the purpose of enabling my agent to carry out the agent's duties toward me, as determined by my agent, including (but not limited to) making a determination as to my incapacity for purposes of establishing my agent's authority to act on my behalf. I intend that my agent shall be treated as I would be regarding the use and disclosure of my medical records.

Persons authorized. The persons or entities who are authorized to disclose and release my medical records to my agent are my treating physicians and any other person, entity, or entities who is or are in possession of my medical records and subject to the privacy requirements of the Health Insurance Portability and Accountability Act of 1996 (HIPAA), 42 U.S.C. Section 1320d and 45 CFR parts 160, 164, or any successor legislation, and the California Confidentiality of Medical Information Act, Civil Code Sections 56 to 56.37, or any successor legislation.

Effective date and duration. This authorization is effective immediately. It will remain in effect until one year after my death, unless terminated earlier by operation of law or revoked by me.

Sample HIPAA Release (continued)

Right to revoke. I understand that I may revoke this authorization at any time by signing a written statement of revocation and delivering it to any person acting as my agent or to any physician or entity holding my protected health information. I also understand that any such revocation will not be effective with regard to any protected health information released to my agent by any person acting in good-faith reliance on this authorization without actual knowledge of the revocation.

No conditions imposed. I understand that a person or entity covered by this authorization may in limited circumstances legally condition treatment, payment, enrollment, or eligibility for benefits on whether I sign an authorization. I am signing this authorization for the purpose of planning for incapacity and not as a condition imposed by any person or entity.

Redisclosure of information. My agent may not redisclose my protected health care information except as required or permitted by law. I understand that any information redisclosed by my agent may no longer be protected by HIPAA regulations.

Release from liability. I release any person relying on this authorization from any liability arising from the release of my medical records to my agent in reliance on this authorization while it is in effect.

Copies. A copy of this authorization may be used in place and instead of the original.

Date: _November 2, 20xx_

Signature: _Alice Murphy_

Printed Name: _Alice Murphy_

Sample HIPAA Release (continued)

Certificate of Acknowledgment of Notary Public

A notary public or other officer completing this certificate verifies only the identity of the individual who signed the document to which this certificate is attached, and not the truthfulness, accuracy, or validity of that document.

State of California

County of ___Orange___   } ss

On ___November 2,___ , ___20xx___ , before me, ___Joseph Albertson___ , personally appeared ___Alice Murphy___ , who proved to me on the basis of satisfactory evidence to be the person(s) whose name(s) is/are subscribed to the within instrument and acknowledged to me that he/she/they executed the same in his/her/their authorized capacity(ies), and that by his/her/their signature(s) on the instrument the person(s), or the entity upon behalf of which the person(s) acted, executed the instrument.

I certify under PENALTY OF PERJURY under the laws of the State of California that the foregoing paragraph is true and correct.

WITNESS my hand and official seal.

Joseph Albertson
Notary Public for the State of California

[NOTARY SEAL]   My commission expires ___April 13, 20xx___

Sample Physician's Determination of Incapacity

Physician's Determination of Incapacity

I, _____Jennifer Frank_____ ,

of the City of _____Orange_____ ,

County of _____Orange_____ ,

State of California, declare under penalty of perjury that:

1. I am a physician licensed to practice in the state of California.

2. I examined ____Alice Murphy_____

    on _____February 12_____ , _____20xx_____ . It is my professional opinion that

    _____Alice Murphy_____

    is currently incapacitated and unable to manage his/her finances and property.

Dated: _____February 12, 20xx_____

_____*Jennifer Frank*_____
Signature of Physician

_____Jennifer Frank_____ , Physician

Certificate of Acknowledgment of Notary Public

A notary public or other officer completing this certificate verifies only the identity of the individual who signed the document to which this certificate is attached, and not the truthfulness, accuracy, or validity of that document.

State of California

} ss

County of __Orange_____

On _February 12,_____ , ___20xx___ , before

me, _____Joseph Albertson_____ ,

personally appeared _____Jennifer Frank_____ , who proved to me on the basis of satisfactory evidence to be the person(s) whose name(s) is/are subscribed to the within instrument and acknowledged to me that he/she/they executed the same in his/her/their authorized capacity(ies), and that by his/her/their signature(s) on the instrument the person(s), or the entity upon behalf of which the person(s) acted, executed the instrument.

I certify under PENALTY OF PERJURY under the laws of the State of California that the foregoing paragraph is true and correct.

WITNESS my hand and official seal.

_____*Joseph Albertson*_____
Notary Public for the State of California

[NOTARY SEAL]   My commission expires _____April 13, 20xx_____

A court invalidates your power of attorney. Even after you sign a durable power of attorney for finances, if you become incapacitated there is a remote possibility that a disgruntled relative could ask a court to appoint a conservator to manage your financial affairs.

It's rare, but a power of attorney could be ruled invalid if a judge concludes that you were not of sound mind when you signed the durable power of attorney, or that you were the victim of fraud or undue influence. The power of attorney could also be invalidated for a technical error, such as the failure to have your document notarized. If that happens, the judge could appoint a conservator to take over management of your property.

If a court appoints a conservator, the agent becomes accountable to the conservator—not just to you—and the conservator has the power to revoke your durable power of attorney if the court approves. (Cal. Prob. Code § 4206.)

You get divorced or terminate your domestic partnership. In California, if your spouse is your agent and you divorce, your ex-spouse's authority is immediately terminated. (Cal. Prob. Code § 4154(a).) If you named an alternate (successor) agent in your power of attorney, that person takes over as agent. However, if you get divorced, it's best to revoke your durable power of attorney and make a new one.

If you are a member of a registered domestic partnership the same concern applies to you. If you formally end your partnership, be sure to make a new document and name a new agent.

No agent is available. A durable power of attorney must end if there's no one to serve as the agent. To avoid this, you can name an alternate agent who will serve if your first choice can't.

For a bit of extra insurance, you can also allow the alternate agent to choose someone else to take over, if it's ever necessary.

After your death. A durable power of attorney ends when the principal dies. However, if the agent doesn't know of your death and continues to act on your behalf, those actions are still valid. (Cal. Prob. Code § 4152(b).)

If you want your agent to have any authority over winding up your affairs after your death, you must grant that authority in your will or living trust. (See the list of estate planning resources at the end of Chapter 1.)

How Much It Costs

In most instances, the only expense of creating a durable power of attorney is the price of this book and a small fee for a notary to verify your signature on the document. In some situations, however, there may be other costs.

Up-front costs. If you give your agent power over your real estate, you'll need to file (record) your durable power of attorney with the county clerk's office. Recording your document is explained in "Making Your Durable Power of Attorney Legal," below. There is a fee for this service, about $15 for the first page plus a few dollars for each additional page.

Although it's not usually necessary, you may decide that you want a lawyer to review or modify your durable power of attorney. The fee for this service shouldn't be large, at least by lawyers' standards. But you can expect to pay several hundred dollars to have a lawyer review your document. (For help finding a lawyer, see Chapter 5.)

Ongoing costs. If you become incapacitated and someone must handle your financial affairs for you, additional expenses will crop up. But if you have a durable power of attorney, the cost will be less than if a court-appointed conservator has to take over. Additional expenses include:

- **Agent's payment.** If you decide your agent is to be paid for helping you, those fees will be paid from your assets.
- **Fees for accountants and other experts.** If the agent must hire professionals, such as an accountant or a financial adviser, to help with managing your property and finances, their fees will be paid from your assets.

Will Your Power of Attorney Be Accepted?

Durable powers of attorney are common; financial institutions, insurance companies, and government agencies are used to them. Your agent, armed with a signed and notarized power of attorney document, should have no problem getting people to accept his or her authority.

If questions come up when an agent tries to take action under the power of attorney, the agent should be able to deal with them. Here are some issues third parties may raise.

Is the document still valid? It's reasonable for someone to want to make sure that your durable power of attorney hasn't been changed or revoked. As reassurance, your agent can show that person the power of attorney document; it clearly states that any person who receives a copy of the document may accept it without the risk of legal liability unless he or she knows that the document has been revoked.

Under California law, anyone who in good faith relies on a power of attorney that appears to be valid and properly executed can't be sued if the document later turns out to be invalid. (Cal. Prob. Code § 4303.)

Your agent can also sign a sworn statement (an affidavit) in front of a notary public, stating that as far as he or she knows, the durable power of attorney has not been revoked and that you are still alive. Under the law, this statement is sufficient to prove to third parties that the durable power of attorney is still valid. (Cal. Prob. Code § 4305.)

If a third party is unusually stubborn, the agent can point to Section 4406 of the California Probate Code, which states that a third party who receives a properly prepared statutory form power of attorney (the kind contained in this book) must honor the document under any circumstance in which the third party would be required to accept your

own authority. In other words, if your bank is required to let you withdraw funds from an account, it can't refuse your agent's request to do the same when faced with a properly prepared document. If it does, Section 4406 allows your agent to get a court order requiring the bank to accept the power of attorney—and perhaps recover attorneys' fees for the trouble.

Does the agent have the authority he or she claims? Any third party who relies on a durable power of attorney must be sure that the agent has the power he or she claims to have. That means the third party must examine the document, to see what power it grants.

California's power of attorney law is very specific about the agent's powers. For example, if you give your agent authority over your banking transactions, the document indicates this, and the California statutes describe in detail what the agent can do, including:

- managing, changing, or terminating accounts
- withdrawing funds by writing checks or other methods
- receiving bank statements
- obtaining or closing a safe deposit box and adding to or withdrawing from its contents
- borrowing money
- applying for credit cards, and
- changing the terms of bank loans.

If necessary, your agent can point to the statutory section that grants the power in question, so a doubting third party can read it in black and white. (The powers you can grant to your agent are defined in Sections 4451–4463 of the California Probate Code, and are discussed in detail in "Preparing Your Durable Power of Attorney," below.)

An agent who runs into resistance should seek, politely but insistently, someone higher up in the bureaucracy. And, as mentioned above, the agent may want to point out the requirements of Probate Code Section 4406.

Were you of sound mind? If you weren't of sound mind when you signed your durable power, the document has no legal effect. If you are concerned that someone might raise this issue later and demand proof that you knew what you were doing when you signed your durable power, you may want to consult a lawyer as discussed in "The Mental Capacity Requirement" in Chapter 1.

About Your Agent for Finances

This section explains more about the responsibilities the person you name as agent will have toward you and your property. It also offers some guidance to help you choose the right person for the job.

Powers You Can Grant

Commonly, people give their agents broad power over their finances. But you can give your agent as much or as little power as you wish. With the durable power of attorney form in this book, the powers you can give your agent include:

- using your assets to pay your everyday expenses and those of your family
- handling transactions with banks and other financial institutions
- buying, selling, maintaining, paying taxes on, and mortgaging real estate and other property
- filing and paying your taxes
- managing your retirement accounts
- collecting benefits from Social Security, Medicare, other government programs, or civil or military service
- investing your money in stocks, bonds, and mutual funds
- buying and selling insurance policies and annuities for you

- operating your small business
- claiming or disclaiming property you inherit
- hiring someone to represent you in court
- making gifts of your assets to organizations and individuals that you choose, and
- transferring property to a living trust you've already set up.

These powers are discussed in detail in "Preparing Your Durable Power of Attorney," below.

You can also place conditions or restrictions upon the agent. For example, you can give your agent authority over your real estate, but with the express restriction that your house may not be sold.

What Your Agent Can't Do

There are a few powers you can't give to your agent under your durable power of attorney for finances.

Medical decisions. A durable power of attorney for finances does not give your agent legal authority to make health care decisions for you. To make sure that your wishes for medical care are known and followed, you should create medical directives. (See Chapters 2 and 3.)

Marriage, adoption, voting, wills. You cannot authorize your agent to marry, adopt, vote in public elections, or make a will on your behalf. These acts are considered too personal to delegate to someone else.

Powers you've already delegated. If you've already given someone else legal authority to manage some or all of your property, you cannot delegate that authority to your agent. Here are two common examples:

- You created a living trust that gives the successor trustee power over trust property if you become incapacitated, or
- You signed a partnership agreement that gives your partners authority to manage your interest in the business if you can't.

Legal Responsibilities

How much authority you want to give your agent is up to you. But whatever the agent's duties, he or she must always act in your best interests.

Basic Responsibilities: Honesty and Prudence

The agent you appoint in your power of attorney is a "fiduciary"—someone who holds a position of trust and must act in your best interests. Essentially, the law requires your agent to:

- handle your property honestly and prudently
- act in your best interests
- keep your property completely separate from his or her own
- keep you informed and follow your instructions as much as possible under the circumstances
- keep adequate records
- use any special skills that the agent has, and
- deliver your property to the appropriate people when the agent's authority ends.

These legal responsibilities do not present problems in most simple situations. For example, if you just want your agent to sign for your pension check, deposit it in your bank account, and pay for your basic needs, there is slight possibility of uncertainty or dispute.

Sometimes, however, these rules impose unnecessary hardships on an agent. For example, your property may already be mixed with that of your agent, and it may make good sense for that to continue. Fortunately, you can use your power of attorney document to give your agent permission to deviate from some of the rules.

These rules and exceptions are discussed below.

Managing your property prudently. The agent must be careful with your money and other property. California law generally requires an agent to act as a "prudent person" would under the circumstances. (Cal. Prob. Code § 4231(a).)

That means the agent has no obligation to make canny investment moves with your cash. The primary goal is not to lose your money.

The agent may, however, take careful actions on your behalf. For example, if your money is in a low-interest bank account, the agent might invest it in government bonds, which pay higher interest but are still very safe.

As long as your agent acts prudently, the agent is not liable for a well-meaning decision that turned out badly. The agent will be held personally responsible for losses only if he or she is extremely careless with your assets or actually steals from you.

However, some agents may be held to a higher standard than that of a "prudent person." If your agent has special skills or expertise—for example, if he or she is a lawyer or an accountant—the agent is required to meet the standard of care that would be expected of anyone with these skills. A certified financial planner, for instance, will be expected to perform at the level of other financial planners, not at that of ordinary folks without the same expertise. (Cal. Prob. Code § 4231(b).)

Acting in your best interests. When taking action under a power of attorney, California law requires your agent to act solely in your interest and to avoid conflicts of interest. An agent who is acting according to your best interests, however, is not forbidden from benefiting personally from a transaction conducted on your behalf. (Cal. Prob. Code § 4232.)

EXAMPLE: David is the agent for his elderly mother, Irene. After Irene's failing eyesight makes it impossible for her to drive, David decides to sell her car for her and put the money in a certificate of deposit at her bank. After thinking it over, David decides that his family could use another car for their teenage daughter. He looks up the car's current market value to make sure he is paying a fair amount, writes a check, and opens the CD in his mother's name. Finally, he transfers ownership of the vehicle to his daughter. This transaction is most likely acceptable under California law, because David undertakes the transaction primarily to benefit his mother.

Even though California law is somewhat flexible in allowing the agent to benefit personally from transactions conducted under a power of attorney, doing so has the potential to put your agent on shaky ground if someone challenges these actions in court. Activities that create conflicts of interest (or that give the impression of such conflicts) between the principal and agent are called "self-dealing"— and they are likely to draw scrutiny from a court in the event of a dispute over the agent's handling of the principal's affairs. For this reason, it's generally best for agents to avoid self-dealing altogether.

Nevertheless, in some circumstances it makes sense for the agent to have permission to benefit from transactions carried out under a power of attorney—for example, if the agent is your spouse, a close family member, a business partner, or another person whose affairs are already intertwined with yours. For instance, if your agent is also your wife, or your child who will someday inherit most or all of your property, you don't want her to have to worry because selling an item of property you own jointly will benefit her as well as you. In a case like this, you can provide extra protection for your agent by adding a simple clause to your power of attorney that explicitly allows the agent to benefit from transactions conducted on your behalf. We'll show you how to add this clause when you prepare your document.

Keeping funds separate. An agent is not allowed to mix (commingle) your funds with the agent's own. (Cal. Prob. Code § 4233.) However, if you wish, your power of attorney can specifically authorize your agent to commingle funds. You will probably want to grant this authority if you appoint your spouse or partner as agent, and your finances are already thoroughly mixed together in joint bank or security accounts.

> **EXAMPLE:** Jim and Eduardo have been living together for 25 years. They have a joint checking account and share all basic living expenses. Each names the other as his agent in durable power of attorney documents. To avoid any possible problems, Jim and Eduardo both include, in their powers of attorney, specific provisions that allow commingling of funds.

Different Powers for Alternate Agents

Even if you want to give your first-choice agent full power to benefit personally from transactions conducted on your behalf, or to mix your funds with his or hers, you may not feel comfortable giving an alternate agent the same authority. This may be the case if you name your spouse or partner as agent and then name an alternate with whom you are not so closely or financially entwined. In your power of attorney form, you can give your alternate agent the same power as your first choice, or restrict the alternate's authority when it comes to personal benefit and mixing funds.

Keeping you informed and following your instructions. Even after you are incapacitated, your agent must do as much as is reasonable to keep in contact with you and to follow whatever wishes you express about how you want your finances handled. An agent who feels that your judgment is so impaired that your directions are not in your own best interests can ask a court to grant permission to disobey your wishes. (Cal. Prob. Code § 4234.)

Keeping good records. Your agent is legally required to keep accurate and separate records for all transactions made on your behalf. (Cal. Prob. Code § 4236(a).) This is true whether or not the agent is paid to serve as agent. (Paying your agent is discussed below.) Good records are particularly important if the agent ever wants to resign and turn the responsibility over to a successor.

Record keeping isn't an onerous requirement. All the agent must be able to do is show where and how your money has been spent. In most instances, it's enough to have a balanced checkbook and receipts for bills paid and claims made. And because the agent will probably file tax returns on your behalf, income and expense records may be necessary.

You and your prospective agent should discuss and agree on what record keeping is appropriate. The agent may also want to review your current records now to find out where they're kept and to make sure they're in order. If you don't have clear records, the agent may have to spend a lot of time sorting things out later.

As part of managing your finances, the agent may hire a bookkeeper, an accountant, or another financial adviser and pay for the services from your property.

Making Reports

Your agent is not required to provide accountings or reports of transactions made on your behalf unless the power of attorney document requires it or one of the following people requests or orders a report:

- you
- your conservator, if a court appoints one for you
- your personal representative (executor), if you die with a will
- anyone who stands to inherit property from you, if you die without a will, or
- a court.

(Cal. Prob. Code § 4236(b).) The people on this list may also examine and copy any records kept by the agent that relate to the power of attorney. (Cal. Prob. Code § 4236(c).)

RESOURCE

Help getting organized. If, like many people, you keep your records in haphazardly labeled shoeboxes and file folders, this may be a good time to get organized. One way to start is with *Get It Together: Organize Your Records So Your Family Won't Have To*, by Melanie Cullen with Shae Irving (Nolo). The book provides a complete system to help you organize your personal and financial information.

Using special skills. An agent who has any special skills—say your agent happens to be a securities broker or real estate agent—must apply those skills to their full extent when acting on your behalf. (Cal. Prob. Code § 4237.)

Turning over your property. When the agent's authority ends, he or she is required to promptly deliver your property to the appropriate people. (Cal. Prob. Code § 4238(a).) If you are not incapacitated at the time—for example, if you revoke the durable power while you are still of sound mind—this means returning property to you or doing with it whatever you direct. If you are incapacitated, delivering your property may mean giving control to:

- a successor agent
- your spouse, if the property is community property
- a conservator, if one has been appointed, or
- your personal representative (executor), after your death.

If the person taking control of the property requests it, the agent is also required to deliver copies of any transaction records related to the property. (Cal. Prob. Code § 4238(b).)

Supervision of the Agent

An agent is not directly supervised by a court; that's the whole point of appointing one. The agent is not required to file reports with any courts or government agencies unless ordered to do so (see "Making Reports," just above).

If you make a durable power of attorney and become incapacitated, a court may become involved only if someone close to you fears that the agent is acting dishonestly or not in your best interests. It's rare, but close relatives or friends may ask a court to order the agent to take certain actions. Or they may ask the court to terminate the power of attorney and appoint a conservator to look after your affairs. (As mentioned earlier, if a conservator is appointed for you, the agent will have to account to the conservator—or the conservator may get court approval to revoke the durable power of attorney altogether.) Disgruntled family members or friends may also challenge the durable power of attorney on the grounds that you weren't of sound mind when you signed it or were the victim of some kind of fraud.

California law specifically authorizes anyone who is concerned to ask a court to resolve questions about a power of attorney, including whether the document is valid or whether the agent is acting properly under it. (Cal. Prob. Code §§ 4540, 4541.)

Resignation

No one can be forced to serve as an agent—it's a voluntary job, and in theory, the agent can resign at any time. (Cal. Prob. Code § 4207.) Resignation is simplest when the durable power names a successor to take over as agent, and the successor is willing and able to serve.

If your agent resigns after you are incapacitated and your document doesn't name a successor, or the successor cannot serve, a conservatorship proceeding may be necessary. In some circumstances, leaving a disabled principal in the lurch could be considered a breach of duty, and a court might order an agent to continue serving until a conservator is appointed and takes over. (Cal. Prob. Code § 4541.)

Choosing Your Agent

The most important decision you must make when you create a financial power of attorney is who will serve as your agent.

Depending on the powers you grant, the agent may have tremendous power over your property. You need to choose someone you trust completely. Fortunately, most of us know at least one such person—usually a spouse, partner, relative, or close friend. Or, perhaps one member of your family is particularly good at managing business affairs and routinely helps you and other family members with them. If there's no one you trust completely with this great authority, a financial power of attorney isn't for you.

Remember that no one will be keeping an eye on the agent. If your agent handles your affairs carelessly or dishonestly while you are incapacitated, the only recourse of your family or friends would be a lawsuit—obviously, not a satisfactory approach. Lawsuits are burdensome and expensive, and would entangle your loved ones in all the legal red tape a power of attorney is designed to avoid. And there's no guarantee that money lost by a bungling agent would ever be recovered. All this is not said to frighten you needlessly, but simply to underscore the need to make a careful choice.

If you are of sound mind, you can always "fire" a troublesome or dishonest agent by revoking the power of attorney document. But choosing wisely from the start will help you avoid both hard feelings and monetary losses.

General Considerations

Any adult can serve as your agent. But don't appoint someone without first discussing the job with that person and making sure he or she accepts this serious responsibility.

In most situations, the agent does not need extensive experience in financial management; common sense, dependability, and complete honesty are enough. If necessary, your agent can get professional help—from an accountant, a lawyer, or a tax preparer, perhaps—and pay for it out of your assets. If, however, you want the agent to help run your small business or manage extensive investments, be sure you choose someone with enough experience to handle the job.

It's also a good idea to name someone who lives nearby, if possible. Your agent will be responsible for taking care of the day-to-day details of your finances: opening mail, paying bills, looking after property, and so on. Of course, many families are spread across the country these days. If there's only one person you trust enough to name as agent and that person lives far away, you may have to settle for the less than ideal situation.

Sometimes it's tough to know whom to choose. Perhaps your mate is ill or wouldn't be a good choice for other reasons. Or you may not know anyone you feel entirely comfortable asking to take over your financial affairs. Or, if you have an active, complex investment portfolio or own a business, you might decide that your agent needs business skills, knowledge, or management abilities beyond those of the people closest to you.

If you're not sure whom to choose, read the rest of this section and discuss the issue with people you trust. It's better not to make a power of attorney than to turn over your affairs to someone in whom you don't have complete confidence.

CAUTION

Family conflicts can disrupt the handling of your affairs. Long-standing feuds among family members may result in objections to your choice of agent or the extent of the authority you delegate. This can wreak havoc with your agent's ability to handle tasks for you. If you foresee such personal conflicts, it's wise to try to defuse them in advance. A discussion with the people who are leery of the power of attorney might help. If you still feel uncomfortable after talking things over, you may want to discuss the troubles with a knowledgeable lawyer. A lawyer can review your estate planning documents and might help you feel reassured that your plans will be carried out as you wish.

Many Jobs, One Agent	
Job	**Duties**
Agent under your durable power of attorney for finances	Manages your finances if you are incapacitated
Agent under your advance directive for health care	Directs your health care if you are incapacitated; if you choose, your health care agent also decides where you will live and handles the disposition of your body after your death
Executor of your will (called your "personal representative" in California)	Winds up your affairs after your death, including paying debts and distributing property to the people who inherit it
Successor trustee of your living trust, if you have one	Manages trust property if you become incapacitated and distributes it after your death

If You're Married or in a Registered Domestic Partnership

You'll probably want to make your spouse or partner your agent unless there is a compelling reason not to. There are powerful legal and practical reasons, in addition to the emotional ones, for appointing your spouse or registered domestic partner. The main one is that naming anyone else creates the risk of conflicts between the agent and your spouse or partner over how to manage property that belongs to both of you. (The authority of a spouse or partner over your property, if you become incapacitated, is discussed in Chapter 1.)

EXAMPLE: Henry and Amelia, a married couple, each create a durable power of attorney for finances. Henry names Amelia as his agent, but Amelia names her sister Anna. Later, Amelia becomes unable to manage her affairs, and Anna takes over as her agent. Soon Anna and Henry are arguing bitterly over what should be done with the house and investments that Henry and Amelia own together. If they can't resolve their differences, Henry or Anna may have to go to court and ask a judge to determine what is in Amelia's best interests.

If your spouse or partner is ill or otherwise not equipped to manage your financial affairs, you may have to name someone else as agent. The wisest course is for you and your mate to agree on who the agent should be, perhaps one of your grown children.

Remember that if your spouse or partner is your agent, that designation automatically ends if you get divorced. After a divorce you should revoke your power of attorney and create a new one, naming someone else as your new agent.

If You Make an Advance Health Care Directive

To name someone who will make medical decisions on your behalf, you must prepare an advance health care directive (see Chapter 2). It's usually a good idea to name the same person as both your agent for finances and your agent for health care under your advance directive. If that's not practical for some reason, make sure you name agents who get along well and will be able to work together; they may have to do so often. For example, if you need medical care, your health care agent will have to turn to your financial agent to be sure insurance matters are handled and medical bills are paid.

If You Have a Living Trust

If you have created a revocable living trust to avoid probate or minimize estate taxes, the successor trustee you named in the trust document will have power over the trust property if you become incapacitated. Or, if you and your spouse or partner made a living trust together, the trust document almost certainly gives your mate authority over trust property if you become incapacitated. (Living trusts are discussed in Chapter 1.)

Creating a financial power of attorney doesn't change any of this. Your agent will not have authority over property held in your living trust. To avoid conflicts, it's advisable to name the same person to manage both trust property and nontrust property if you become incapacitated.

> **EXAMPLE:** Carlos, a widower, prepares a revocable living trust to avoid probate and a durable power of attorney for finances in case he becomes incapacitated. He names his son, Jeffrey, as both successor trustee of the living trust and agent under the durable power of attorney.
>
> Several years later, Carlos has a stroke and is temporarily unable to handle his everyday finances. Jeffrey steps in to deposit his father's pension checks and pay his monthly bills, using his authority as agent. As successor trustee, he also has legal authority over the property Carlos holds in his living trust, including Carlos's house.

Appointing More Than One Person

In general, it's a bad idea to name more than one agent, because conflicts between them could disrupt the handling of your finances. Also, some banks and other financial institutions prefer to deal with a single agent.

If you're tempted to name more than one person simply so that no one feels hurt or left out, think again. It may be better to pick one person for the job and explain your choice to your loved ones now. If you name more than one person and they don't get along, they may wind up resolving their disputes in court. This might result in more bad feelings than if you had just picked one person to be agent, and explained your choice, in the first place.

How multiple agents make decisions. If you name more than one agent, you'll have to grapple with the question of how they should make their decisions. You can require co-agents to carry out their duties in one of two ways:

- they must all agree before they take any action on your behalf, or
- they may make decisions independent of one another.

Both methods have strengths and pitfalls. Requiring your agents to act jointly ensures that decisions are made carefully and with the knowledge of everyone involved, but coordinating multiple decision makers can be burdensome and time-consuming. On the other hand, allowing your agents to act separately makes it easy to get things done, but can lead to poor record keeping and general confusion. For example, one agent could independently take money out of your bank accounts or sell stock without full knowledge of what the other is doing to manage your investments.

There's no hard-and-fast rule on which strategy is better. Choose the method that feels most comfortable to you.

If your agents disagree. Your agents can decide how to handle the matter, keeping in mind that their foremost responsibility is to act in your best interest. But if your agents get into a dispute that interferes with their ability to represent you properly, they may need help working things out. Getting help could mean hiring a mediator—or going to court to have a judge decide what's best. The downside of all this is not just that there could be confusion and delays in handling your finances, but also that you'll probably be the one to pay the costs of settling the dispute.

If one or more of your agents can't serve. If you name more than one agent, and one of them can't serve, the others will continue to serve. If none of them can serve, an alternate can take over. (See below for more information about naming an alternate agent.)

If You Can't Think of Anyone to Name

If you can't come up with a family member or close friend to name, you may want to consider asking your lawyer, business partner, or banker to serve as agent. If you really know and trust the person, it may be a good option for you. You may also want to consider naming a professional fiduciary, a person you contract with to serve as your agent for finances. To find and interview professional fiduciaries in your area, visit the website of the National Guardianship Association at www.guardianship.org. Once there, click "Find a Guardian" at the top of the page, then scroll down to the last option, "Search by Zip Code and Distance." Enter your zip code and select a range of miles, then choose "Find Zip Codes."

Don't name an institution, such as a bank, as agent. Though California law permits it, it's definitely not desirable. Serving as agent is a personal responsibility, and there should be personal connection and trust between you and your agent. If the person you trust most happens to be your banker, appoint that person, not the bank.

Naming an Alternate Agent

It's a good idea to name someone who will take over as your agent in case your first choice can't serve or needs to resign after serving for a period of time. Your alternate will take over if your initial choice can't serve.

When naming an alternate, use the same criteria that you used to make your first choice for agent. Your alternate should be every bit as trustworthy and competent. If you don't know anyone you trust well enough, skip the matter altogether.

If You Name More Than One Agent

If you name more than one agent, the person you name as alternate will take over only if all of your agents must give up the job. If any of your first choices can continue to serve, they may do so alone, without the addition of your alternate.

As a further precaution, you can authorize your agent to appoint someone to serve if those you named cannot. You do this by giving your agent permission to delegate tasks to others. (We show you how below.) Allowing your agent to delegate authority to someone else eliminates the minimal risk that the position might become vacant because of the original agent's death, disability, or resignation. If this occurs, and you haven't named an alternate or your alternate is not available, your power of attorney would be useless. If you were incapacitated, there would have to be a court action, such as a full-scale conservatorship proceeding, to find someone to manage your affairs.

Paying Your Agent

Under California law, an agent is entitled to reasonable compensation and to reimbursement for reasonable expenses incurred on your behalf. (Cal. Prob. Code § 4204.) However, in family situations, an agent is normally not paid if the duties won't be complicated or burdensome.

If, on the other hand, your property and finances are extensive and the agent is likely to devote significant time and effort to managing them, compensation may be fair—and you can probably afford it. (Keep in mind, however, that an agent who is paid is also held to a higher standard of care when looking after your finances; see "Legal Responsibilities," above.) You should discuss and resolve the issue of payment with the proposed agent before you finalize your document.

If you decide to pay your agent, it's wise to specify the payment arrangement in your power of attorney form. (We show you how to do this in "Compensation and Reimbursement of Agent," below.) You can set your own rate—for example, $10,000 per year, $30 per hour, or some other figure that you and your agent agree on. Or, if you don't want to decide on an amount right now, you can allow your agent to determine a reasonable wage if it seems appropriate. No single strategy works best for everyone. Choose the approach—and the amount—that feels right to you.

> **EXAMPLE 1:** Frederick is quite wealthy. He owns and operates a successful chain of convenience stores in a large city. He also owns a house, several pieces of investment property, and a wide array of stocks. When he is diagnosed with a life-threatening illness, he creates a durable power of attorney appointing his close friend Barbara as his agent. Because he expects Barbara to watch over his business as well as tend to his other financial affairs, he feels it's appropriate to pay her for her services. Frederick and Barbara settle on a rate of $30,000 per year for her services.

> **EXAMPLE 2:** Martin creates a springing durable power of attorney naming his brother, Andrew, as agent. Martin owns a complex investment portfolio, and the brothers agree that Andrew should be paid if he has to manage Martin's finances. They consider an hourly wage, but decide not to be that specific now. In his durable power of attorney, Martin states that Andrew may pay himself reasonable fees for his services if they're ever necessary.

If You Name More Than One Agent

If you name more than one agent and you want to pay them, your document may specify that each is to receive the same amount—for example, $7,000 per year or $25 per hour—or you may set separate rates of pay for each. If you allow your agents to determine a reasonable amount for their services, each will set his or her own salary.

Preparing Your Durable Power of Attorney

California provides a fill-in-the-blanks durable power of attorney form called the "Uniform Statutory Form Power of Attorney." It's called a "statutory form" because you can find the exact text of the form in the California statutes (Section 4401 of the California Probate Code). This type of form is also known as a "short form" because the form itself doesn't include all the details of the authority granted to the agent. Instead, the form lists 13 broad powers (discussed in detail below). You choose the powers you want your agent to have; the details of each are spelled out in the California statutes. (Cal. Prob. Code §§ 4451–4463.)

The California statutory form is fairly straightforward and easy to complete. This section takes you through the form step by step and shows you a completed sample.

Getting Started

This book offers the California statutory power of attorney form as a tear-out form in Appendix B or as a download from Nolo's website (see Appendix A for the link). If you use the downloadable form, just use your word processing program to complete and customize it, following the instructions below.

If you use the tear-out version, start by making a few photocopies of the blank form. You can use one for a draft and save a clean one for the final document—the one you will sign and have notarized. If you fill out the form by hand, be sure to print legibly and use black ink.

Your completed form should not contain any words that have been erased or whited out. If the instructions tell you to cross out something, type a string of x's through the words or draw a straight line through them.

TIP

Making a custom document with the downloadable form. You will find it easier to customize your form if you use the downloadable form on Nolo's website; this is especially true if you want to add quite a few of the special instructions discussed below. (The printed statutory form provides a relatively small space for additional instructions. If you run out of room, you'll have to retype the entire form.) If you want to make a custom form using the website download, follow the link in Appendix A and choose the file PowAttorney.rtf. Open the form with a word processing program and type the clauses you want into the special instructions section. It's important that you open the downloadable RTF files with your word processing program. If you open them directly, some of the legally required formatting in the form will be lost.

SEE AN EXPERT

Get help if you need it. A durable power of attorney can transfer tremendous power either now or, in the case of a springing power of attorney, sometime in the future. Even though you can revoke your document at any time (as long as you are of sound mind), never create a durable power of attorney unless you thoroughly understand what you are doing. If you have questions, see an expert. (See Chapter 5 if you need help finding a lawyer.)

Your Name and Address

In the first blank on the form, enter your name and residence address. Enter your name as it appears on official documents such as your driver's license, bank accounts, or real estate deeds. This may or may not be the name on your birth certificate. Enter it first, middle (if you choose), then last.

EXAMPLE: Your birth certificate lists your name as Rose Ellen Green. But you've always gone by Ellen and always sign documents as Ellen McNee, your married name. You should use Ellen McNee on your durable power of attorney.

Be sure to enter all names in which you hold bank accounts, stocks, bonds, real estate, and other property. This will make things far easier for your agent. If you're including more than one name, enter your full legal name first, followed by "aka" (also known as), then enter your other names.

Making Your Records Consistent

If you use more than one name and you're up for some extra work, consider settling on one name, entering it on your power of attorney form and then changing your other documents to conform. This will clean up your records and save your agent some trouble later on. To change your name on official documents and records—for example, bank accounts, deeds, or Social Security records—you'll have to contact the appropriate government office or financial institution to find out what documentation they'll need to make the change for you.

Naming Your Agent

In the second blank, after the word "appoint," insert the name and address of the person (or people) who will serve as your agent(s) for finances. (A reminder: It's almost always a bad idea to name more than one agent. See "Appointing More Than One Person," above.)

It's also a good idea to name an alternate agent in case your first choice can't serve. You must use the "Special Instructions" part of the form to name an alternate. (See "Adding Special Instructions," below.)

Granting Powers to Your Agent

The next section of the form lists 13 powers. You can give your agent all of them or only some. Either way, you can put specific limitations on the powers that you grant. For example, if you give your agent authority over your real estate, you can still add special instructions forbidding the agent from selling your residence.

Scanning the list of powers, you may think it's not necessary to grant some of them—after all, why give your agent authority over "claims and litigation" when you aren't involved in any lawsuits? What you should keep in mind is that even though you aren't involved in a lawsuit now, you could be later. For example, your power of attorney might spring into effect because you're in the hospital, seriously injured in a car accident, and you can't take care of your financial affairs. Your agent might need authority to settle a claim on your behalf.

If you, like most people, want to give your agent every power on the list, initial the blank in front of line (N) and skip to the "Special Instructions" part of the form. (See "Adding Special Instructions," below.) If you want to give only some powers, initial the blank in front of each power you want to grant. You can cross out the others, but it's not required.

The rest of this section discusses and describes each power in turn. (They are lettered as they appear in the form itself.) It describes the actions that agents commonly take under the powers and flags anything about a power that might seem extreme or cause concern—for example, the agent's ability to change beneficiary designations under your retirement plans. This should help you understand the powers and decide which ones you feel comfortable giving to your agent.

RESOURCE

More details about the agent's powers.
This section doesn't cover every possible action
your agent could take under each power. Each of
the powers is described in greater (and sometimes
excruciating) detail in Sections 4451–4463 of the
California Probate Code.

(A) Real Property Transactions

This power puts the agent in charge of managing
any real estate you own. Your agent must, for
example, pay your mortgage and taxes (with
your assets) and arrange for necessary repairs and
maintenance. Most important, the agent may
sell, mortgage, partition, or lease your real estate.

The agent may also take any other action connected to real estate. For example, your agent may:

- buy or lease real estate for you
- refinance your mortgage to get a better
  interest rate
- pay off liens (legal claims) on your property
- buy insurance for your property
- build, remodel, or remove structures on
  your property
- grant easements over your property, and
- bring or defend lawsuits over real estate.

Remember, however, that the agent has a
legal obligation to take only those actions that
are in your best interests.

(B) Tangible Personal Property Transactions

Tangible personal property means physical
items—for example, cars, furniture, jewelry,
computers, and stereo equipment. It does not
include real estate or intangible property such
as stocks or bank notes. If you grant this power,
your agent can buy, sell, rent, or exchange
personal property on your behalf. Your agent
can also insure, use, move, store, repair, or pawn
your personal things. Again, all actions must be
taken in your best interest.

EXAMPLE: Paul names his wife, Gloria, as his
agent for financial matters. When he later goes
into a nursing home, his old car, which he can no
longer use, becomes an expense Gloria cannot
afford. As Paul's agent, she has legal authority
to sell the car and use the proceeds to help take
care of him.

(C) Stock and Bond Transactions

This power gives your agent the power to buy,
sell, or exchange securities for you, including
stocks, bonds, mutual funds, certificates
of deposit, and almost all other financial
instruments. (The exceptions are commodity
fixtures contracts and call-and-put options on
stocks or stock indexes, discussed just below.)
Your agent can buy or sell securities on your
behalf, accept or transfer certificates or other
evidence of ownership, and exercise voting rights.

CAUTION

**Brokers may have their own power of
attorney forms.** Many brokerage houses have their
own power of attorney forms. If yours does, it's a
good idea to use it in addition to your statutory
power of attorney. Using your broker's form will make
things easier for your agent because your broker will
have no need to investigate your power of attorney
or quibble over its terms. The broker will already have
its form on file and will understand exactly what your
agent is authorized to do.

(D) Commodity and Option Transactions

Most people aren't involved in commodity
trading, but if you are, this power lets your agent
buy, sell, exchange, assign, settle, or exercise
options and commodities, and set up, manage,
or terminate option accounts with a broker. It
gives your agent the power to handle commodity
futures contracts and stock call-and-put options
traded on a regulated option exchange.

(E) Banking and Other Financial Institution Transactions

One of the most common reasons for making a power of attorney is to arrange for someone to handle banking transactions. If you give your agent authority to handle your bank accounts, your bills can be paid, and pension or other checks can be deposited in your accounts even if you are not able to take care of these matters yourself.

> **EXAMPLE:** Virginia, who is in her 70s, is admitted to the hospital for emergency surgery. She's too weak to even think about paying her bills or depositing her Social Security check—and anyway, she can't get to the bank. Fortunately, she earlier created a durable power of attorney for finances, naming her niece Marianne as her agent. Marianne can deposit Virginia's Social Security benefits and sign checks to pay the bills that come while Virginia is in the hospital.

Your agent may open and close accounts with banks, savings and loans, credit unions, or other financial institutions on your behalf. The agent may write checks on these accounts, endorse checks you receive, and receive account statements. The agent also has access to your safe deposit box, to withdraw or add to its contents. He or she may also borrow money on your behalf, and pledge your assets as security for the loan.

Signing Checks and Other Documents

Many people wonder how the agent signs checks and other documents on behalf of the principal. Exact procedures vary depending on the financial institution or government agency. Typically, however, after visiting or contacting a particular institution or agency to establish his or her authority, the agent will first sign your name and then his or her own name to checks and documents, followed by words such as "under power of attorney dated June 15, 20xx" or simply, "POA."

 CAUTION

Ask your financial institutions about their power of attorney forms. Many banks and other financial institutions have their own power of attorney forms. Even though granting the banking power will give your agent authority to act on your behalf at any financial institution, it's a good idea to use the financial institution's form in addition to the statutory form. Using the form that your financial institution is most familiar with may make it easier for your agent to get things done.

(F) Business Operating Transactions

This power gives your agent authority to act for you in operating a business that you own yourself or that you run with other people. Subject to the terms of any partnership agreement, limited liability company operating agreement, or corporate rules (bylaws and shareholders' agreements), your agent may:

- sell or liquidate the business
- merge with another company
- prepare, sign, and file reports, information, and returns with government agencies
- pay business taxes
- enforce the terms of a partnership agreement, if any, in court, and
- exercise any power or option you have under a partnership agreement.

If your business is a sole proprietorship, the agent may also:

- hire and fire employees
- move the business
- change the nature of the business or its methods of operation, including selling, marketing, accounting, and advertising
- change the name of the business
- change the form of the business's organization—that is, enter into a partnership agreement or incorporate the business
- continue or renegotiate the business's contracts
- hire lawyers, accountants, or others, and
- collect and spend money on behalf of the business.

If you're a sole proprietor, a power of attorney is a very useful way to let someone else run the business if you're unable to do so, either for a short time or due to incapacity. Be sure to work out a business plan with the person you intend to appoint as your agent; explain what you want for your business and how you expect it to be managed.

If you operate your business with other people as a partnership, limited liability company, or closely held corporation, your business agreement should cover what happens if a partner or shareholder becomes unavailable. Typically, the other business owners can operate the business during your absence or even buy out your share. These rules can't be overridden by a power of attorney. So carefully check your partnership agreement, operating agreement, or corporate bylaws and shareholders' agreements.

> **EXAMPLE:** Mike wants his wife, Nancy, to be his agent to manage his finances if he becomes incapacitated. Mike, a house painter, runs the M-J Painting Company with his equal partner, Jack. Mike and Jack's partnership agreement provides that if one partner becomes incapacitated, the other has exclusive authority to operate the business.
>
> Mike, Jack, and Nancy should think through the arrangement carefully; if Jack and Nancy have conflicts over money, there could be problems. Whatever they decide on should be spelled out in detail in the partnership agreement. They may also want to create a customized durable power of attorney, with a lawyer's help, that sets out the details of the business arrangements.

(G) Insurance and Annuity Transactions

This power allows your agent to buy, borrow against, cash in, or cancel insurance policies or annuity contracts for you and your spouse, registered domestic partner, children, and other dependent family members. The agent's authority extends to all policies and contracts you own, whether they name you or someone else as the beneficiary. (Beneficiaries are the people who will receive the proceeds of the policy when you die.)

The one exception to this rule covers any insurance policies you own with your spouse or registered domestic partner. Under these policies, your spouse or partner must consent to any transaction that affects the policy. So if your agent is not your spouse, he or she will have to obtain your mate's permission before taking action. In California, a community property state (meaning that most property acquired during marriage belongs to both spouses or registered partners), policies that are in one person's name may in fact be owned by both. If you have questions about who owns your insurance policies, consult a lawyer.

If you already have an insurance policy or annuity contract, your agent can keep paying the premiums or cancel the policy, whichever he or she decides is in your best interests.

Your agent is also permitted to name—or change—the beneficiaries of your insurance policies or annuity contracts. This is a broad power, and it's a good idea to discuss your wishes about it with your agent. If you don't want your agent to change your beneficiary designations, you should make that clear in the special instructions part of your form. If you have strong feelings about who the beneficiary of any new policies should be, you can discuss that as well.

There is one important limitation on your agent's ability to designate beneficiaries. Your agent may name himself or herself as a beneficiary of a new policy, or as a beneficiary on a renewal of, extension of, or substitute for an existing policy, only to the extent that he or she was beneficiary before you signed the power of attorney.

(H) Estate, Trust, and Other Beneficiary Transactions

This power primarily authorizes your agent to act on your behalf to claim or disclaim (give up) property you inherit or are entitled to from any other source. But it also gives your agent the important power to transfer items of property into your living trust, if you have created one.

Claiming or disclaiming property. If you are entitled to inherit property or receive money from another source—a trust fund, for example —your agent can make your claim for you. Or, if you don't really need the money, your agent could turn down the cash. (Of course, your agent can't turn away property you inherit unless he or she feels that it's in your best interest to do so.)

Your agent is also entitled to watch out for your interests with regard to the property you stand to receive. This means, for example, that the agent can initiate legal proceedings on your behalf to clarify your rights to the property or to question improper actions of whoever is in charge of the assets.

Living trust transactions. A revocable living trust is a legal structure you create by preparing and signing a document that specifies who will receive certain property at your death. In this way, it operates much like a will. Unlike a will, however, property in a living trust avoids the cost and delay of probate. Certain kinds of trusts also help you save on estate taxes.

If you've already set up a revocable living trust to avoid probate or estate taxes, this power gives your agent the authority to transfer items of your property to that trust. But your agent can transfer an item of property into your trust only if you've given the agent authority over that kind of property elsewhere in your document. For example, if you want your agent to be able to transfer real estate into your living trust, you must also grant Power (A), which gives your agent full power over your real estate. Or, if you want your agent to have authority to transfer bank accounts to your living trust, you must also grant Power (E), the banking transactions power.

> **EXAMPLE:** Maureen sets up a revocable living trust to avoid probate at her death, and holds her house and some valuable antiques in the trust. She also makes a durable power of attorney for finances. Years later, when Maureen becomes incapacitated from a stroke, her son Paul takes over as her agent. While she is incapacitated, Maureen inherits a house from her elder sister. Paul, as agent, is able to transfer the house to Maureen's living trust—avoiding substantial probate hassles for Maureen's heirs when she dies.

For information about granting your agent additional powers over a living trust, including the power to create, change, or revoke a trust, see "Adding Special Instructions," below.

(I) Claims and Litigation

This provision allows your agent to act for you in all matters that involve courts or government agencies. For example, your agent can bring or settle a lawsuit on your behalf. He or she can also accept court papers intended for you, and hire an attorney to represent you in court, if necessary. (Unless your agent is a lawyer, he or she may not actually represent you in court, but must hire someone to do so.) If you lose a lawsuit, the agent can use your assets to pay the winner whatever you are obligated to pay.

(J) Personal and Family Maintenance

This is an important power. It gives the agent the authority to use your assets to pay your everyday expenses and those of your family. The agent can spend your money for your family's food, living quarters, education, cars, medical and dental care, membership dues (for churches, clubs, or other organizations), vacations, and travel. The agent is allowed to spend as much as it takes to maintain your customary standard of living and that of your spouse, children, and anyone else you usually support.

What About Your Pets?

Legally speaking, your pets are property. From an emotional perspective, however, they may feel like members of your family. Chances are good that a properly executed power of attorney that includes all the standard powers would permit your agent to spend money to take care of your pets. But because the law isn't explicit about pets, you may want to add special instructions to your form to ensure that your agent has complete authority to provide care for your animals. For suggested language, see the sample clauses in the "Adding Special Instructions" section, below.

You may normally support people other than your legal dependents. If you regularly take care of others—for example, you are the primary caretaker of a disabled sibling or an aging parent—your agent can use your assets to continue to help those people. You should talk with your agent and explain exactly what your support obligations are. If you like, you can write out specific guidelines in the special instructions part of your form.

(K) Benefits From Social Security, Medicare, Medicaid, or Other Governmental Programs, or Civil or Military Service

This power allows your agent to apply for, collect, and manage any government benefits you may be entitled to, from Social Security, Medicare, Medicaid, or other governmental programs, or from civil or military service. To collect most government benefits, your agent must send the government office a copy of the financial power of attorney. The Social Security Administration, however, requires more proof of authority. (See "Social Security Checks," below.)

Social Security Checks

To collect your Social Security benefits, your agent will have to take the power of attorney document to a local Social Security office. Someone there will interview the agent and establish him or her as your "representative payee"—that is, someone entitled to receive your Social Security checks for you.

If you're creating a power of attorney that's effective immediately, you can save your agent some work by simply contacting the Social Security Administration (SSA) now and naming your agent as your representative payee. However, that means your agent will start receiving your Social Security checks right away, and you may not want that. If it's not yet time for the agent to take control, you're better off granting the "government benefits" power and letting the agent deal with the Social Security Administration if the time comes.

In addition to granting the government benefits power, you might also consider having your Social Security check deposited directly into a bank account where your agent will have access to the funds without the hassles of dealing with the SSA. To learn more about the representative payee's job, visit the Social Security website at www.socialsecurity.gov/payee/faqrep.htm.

To appoint a representative payee or arrange for direct deposit of your benefits, contact the SSA at 800-772-1213.

(L) Retirement Plan Transactions

This power gives your agent authority over retirement plans such as pensions and IRAs. The agent may select payment options, designate beneficiaries (the people who will inherit any money left in the fund at your death) and change current beneficiary designations, make voluntary contributions to (and mandatory withdrawals from) your plan, change the way the funds are invested, and roll over plan benefits into other retirement plans. If authorized by the plan, the agent may make withdrawals or borrow from, sell assets to, and buy assets from the plan.

Be aware of how broad some of these powers are. For example, the power to change the beneficiaries of your retirement funds is a drastic one. You should talk with your agent to make your wishes clear with respect to this power.

(M) Tax Matters

This provision gives your agent authority to act for you in all state, local, federal, and foreign tax matters. The agent can prepare and file tax returns and other documents, pay tax you owe, contest tax bills, and collect refunds. (To file a tax return on your behalf, the agent must include a copy of the power of attorney with the return.) The agent is also authorized to receive confidential information from the IRS. (Cal. Prob. Code § 4235.)

The IRS Power of Attorney Form

The IRS has its own power of attorney form, but you don't need to use it. It is primarily designed to allow attorneys, accountants, and other professionals to receive confidential tax information on behalf of clients. It is not a comprehensive, durable power of attorney for tax matters. The power of attorney contained in this book gives your agent the power to receive confidential information from the IRS, plus the authority to handle any tax matters that arise.

Adding Special Instructions

Listed below are many clauses and powers that you might consider adding to the "Special Instructions" section of your durable power of attorney form. Certainly you won't need to use them all; you may not even need any. The most important clauses are the first two: naming an alternate agent and establishing the effective date if you wish to make a springing power of attorney. If you don't include this second provision, your durable power of attorney will take effect as soon as you sign it.

Possible Instructions

The special instructions you add to your form will depend on the particulars of your situation, so it would be impossible to cover every option in this book. This section discusses the types of instructions people are most likely to need:

- naming an alternate agent
- establishing the effective date of your power of attorney
- stating who will determine whether you are incapacitated
- paying your agent
- stating whether your agent may benefit personally under the document
- stating whether your agent may mix (commingle) his or her property with yours
- stating whether your agent may delegate duties to others
- granting additional powers to your agent, including the powers to manage digital assets and accounts; to make gifts of your property; to take care of your pets; or to create, modify, revoke, or fund a trust
- placing limits on the agent's authority
- requiring the agent to make periodic reports to people that you choose, and
- nominating a conservator.

Alternate Agent

This clause permits you to name an alternate agent who will take over if your agent is unable to serve (see "Choosing Your Agent," above).

If _[name of agent]_ does not or ceases to serve as agent, I appoint___ _[name and address of alternate]_ to serve as agent.

Effective Date and Determination of Incapacity

Use the following clause if you wish to make a durable power of attorney that doesn't take effect unless a doctor determines that you're incapacitated (see "When Your Document Becomes Effective," at the beginning of this chapter).

This power of attorney shall take effect only if I become incapacitated or disabled and unable to manage my financial affairs.

If you include this clause, you should also use the following clause to name one or two doctors to determine whether or not you are incapacitated.

For purposes of this durable power of attorney, my incapacity or disability shall be determined by the written declarations of ___ _[insert correct number: "one" or "two"]___ licensed physician[s]. Each declaration shall be made under penalty of perjury and shall state that in the physician's opinion I am substantially unable to manage my financial affairs. No licensed physician shall be liable to me for any actions taken under this paragraph that are done in good faith.

If you wish to name specific doctors to make the determination, add the following sentence to the end of the clause. If you don't use this sentence, your agent will choose the doctor(s) for you.

If possible, the declaration[s] shall be made by ___ _[name of physician(s)]___ .

CAUTION

Remember to prepare your HIPAA release form. If you are making a durable power of attorney that doesn't take effect unless one or two doctors determine that you are incapacitated, you must fill out a release form that authorizes your agent to receive confidential medical information from the doctors. (See the discussion, "Making the Power of Attorney Effective Later," near the beginning of this chapter.) You can find the release form, titled "Authorization for Disclosure and Use of Protected Health Information," as a tear-out form in Appendix B or as a download on Nolo's website (see Appendix A for the link). Complete the form, sign it in front of a notary public, and be sure your agent and any alternate agents know where to find the form if it's ever necessary.

Compensation and Reimbursement of Agent

You can choose any one of the following three clauses to provide reimbursement and compensation for your agent (see "Paying Your Agent," above).

No Compensation; Reimbursement Only

My agent shall not be compensated for services, but shall be entitled to reimbursement, from my assets, for reasonable expenses incurred on my behalf. Reasonable expenses include but are not limited to reasonable fees for information or advice from accountants, lawyers, or investment experts relating to my agent's responsibilities under this power of attorney.

Reasonable Compensation to Be Determined by the Agent

My agent shall be entitled to reimbursement for reasonable expenses and reasonable compensation for services. What constitutes reasonable compensation shall be determined exclusively by my agent. If more than one agent is named in this document, each shall have the exclusive right to determine what constitutes reasonable compensation for his or her own duties.

> ### Reasonable Compensation Stated in the Power of Attorney Document
>
> My agent shall be entitled to reimbursement for reasonable expenses and compensation for services in the amount of $_____ .
> If more than one agent is named in this document, each shall be entitled to receive this amount.

Personal Benefit by Agent

To make clear whether or not your agent is permitted to benefit personally from transactions conducted on your behalf, choose one of the following clauses. If you do not include any of them, your agent will be held to the standards discussed in "Legal Responsibilities," above.

> ### Agent May Benefit Personally
>
> My agent may buy any assets of mine or engage in any transaction he or she deems in good faith to be in my interest, no matter what the interest or benefit to my agent.

> ### Primary Agent May Benefit Personally; Alternate Agent May Not
>
> My agent may buy any assets of mine or engage in any transaction he or she deems in good faith to be in my interest, no matter what the interest or benefit to my agent. However, if an alternate agent is serving under this document, the alternate may not benefit personally from any transaction conducted on my behalf.

> ### Agent May Not Benefit Personally
>
> My agent may not benefit personally from any transaction conducted on my behalf.

If you give your agent the power to make gifts of your property to himself or herself (see below), but don't want the agent to benefit personally in any other way, you should add the following clause to your form:

> ### Agent May Not Benefit Personally Except for Gifts
>
> Although my agent may receive gifts of my property as described in this document, my agent may not benefit personally from any other transaction that he or she conducts on my behalf.

Commingling by Agent

You can choose one of the following clauses to specify your wishes about whether or not the agent may mix your funds with his or her own. If you don't use one of these clauses, the agent is not permitted to commingle funds. (See "Legal Responsibilities," above.)

> ### Agent May Commingle Funds
>
> My agent may commingle any of my funds with any funds of his or hers.

> ### Primary Agent May Commingle Funds; Alternate Agent May Not
>
> My agent may commingle any of my funds with any funds of his or hers. However, if an alternate agent is serving under this document, the alternate may not commingle any of my funds with his or hers.

Delegation of Duties by Agent

If your agent resigns from the job and you named an alternate agent, that person will take over. But if there is no alternate available, or if your agent is only temporarily unavailable, the agent will need to find a stand-in. If you allow it, your agent in this situation can turn over all or part of his or her duties to someone else. This reassignment of duties is called "delegation."

An agent who is allowed to delegate tasks is free to turn over any or all of the job to a competent third person. This person may step in on a temporary basis or permanently, depending on the situation.

If you want to give your agent the power to delegate tasks, add the following clause to your form:

> My agent may delegate, in writing, any authority granted under this power of attorney to a person he or she selects. Any such delegation shall state the period during which it is valid and specify the extent of the delegation.

Digital Assets and Accounts

As this book goes to print, California has not yet passed a law allowing agents to manage digital assets, such as email, online financial accounts, social media profiles, blog accounts, and other electronic accounts or files. If you want your agent to have access to your digital assets, you should add this power to your document and also, in a separate document, provide information for your agent about how to access the accounts—usernames, passwords, and so on. On the other hand, if you know you don't want your agent to have access to your digital assets, skip this power.

If you include the language below in the special instructions section of your power of attorney, your document will give your agent very broad rights, including the right to access, control, distribute, duplicate, or deactivate or delete your accounts or records. Of course, like all authority you grant in your power of attorney, your agent may do these things only in your best interest and according to your instructions.

Ideally, this power will allow your agent to handle tasks like paying bills using your online bank account, posting a note to your blog, or renewing your auto insurance online. But, in the absence of a California law confirming these powers, the statement in your document may not be enough. Your agent's power to get into your accounts will most likely depend on:

- whether your agent has your username and password information, and
- the terms of your agreement with the company that manages the account.

The easiest way to make sure that your agent will be able to access your accounts is to provide your username and password information. That way, your agent will immediately have the same control over your accounts as you would have. You can include this information in a separate document or letter for your agent. Just be sure to store it in a safe place and tell your agent where to find it if the time comes.

Without your login information, even if you add this authority to your power of attorney, your agent may have a hard time getting access to your digital accounts. Even in states that do have laws supporting this power, agents struggle with companies that actively resist turning over account information.

The law in this area is changing rapidly, and procedures for dealing with digital property will surely become clearer in the future. For now, the best you can do is include this power in your power of attorney and write that separate letter so your agent knows how to get into the accounts that matter to you. In that letter, you may also wish to provide some guidance on what you'd like your agent to do with your digital property. For example, you could ask your agent to respond to certain emails, update the amount of your automatic online payments to reflect any annual increases in your bills, or close your Facebook account. For more help thinking about how your agent could help with your digital assets—and to keep up on the status of California's law in this area—go to www.nolo.com/legal-encyclopedia/digital-assets.

Digital Assets Transactions

My agent may act for me as an account holder and authorized user of my digital assets. My agent's powers include but are not limited to access, control, use, transfer, distribution, duplication, deactivation or deletion of my digital assets. My digital assets include but are not limited to email or other electronic communication, personal or professional websites, online banking and other financial accounts, frequent flyer accounts and other reward programs, social media profiles, digital music, photographs or videos, software or any other electronic record or account. To exercise this power, my agent may access and control any device or equipment used by me to store or manage my digital assets, such as desktop computers, laptop computers, tablets, external drives, cell phones or any other device used for access and control of digital assets that currently exists or may exist as technology develops.

Gifts to Agent or Others

You may want your agent to be able to give away your property under some circumstances. On the other hand, allowing your agent to make gifts might feel like giving up too much control. This section helps you decide what makes sense for you.

If you give your agent the authority to make gifts, be sure to discuss your intentions with him or her. Your agent should have a sound understanding of your gift-giving goals, including the recipients you have in mind, under what circumstances gifts should be made, and in what amounts. Remember that any gifts your agent makes must be in your best interest or according to your explicit instructions.

Allowing Your Agent to Make Gifts

There are many reasons why you might want to permit your agent to make gifts of your property. Here are a few of the most common.

If You Named More Than One Agent

Delegation becomes more complicated if you name more than one agent. Here are some issues to think about.

Agents Who Must Act Jointly

If you will require your agents to act together in all that they do, it's a good idea to give them the power to delegate responsibilities. That way, an agent who becomes temporarily unable to act on your behalf can delegate his or her authority to the remaining agents. Your remaining agents can use the written delegation to prove that they are permitted to act alone. If you don't grant the delegation power, an agent who will be unavailable will have to write and sign an affidavit—a sworn, notarized statement—saying that he or she cannot act for you. (An agent who permanently resigns can prepare a resignation form; the remaining agents can use that form to prove their authority.)

In the unlikely event that all of your agents will be temporarily unavailable, they can choose a person to take over if you've given them the power to delegate. Because your agents must act together, they must agree on any person who will take over some or all of their job.

Agents Who May Act Separately

If you've authorized your agents to act independently, allowing them to delegate tasks is probably not necessary or wise. The main reason for allowing delegation is to ensure that someone will always be on hand to take care of your finances. In your situation, if just one of your agents is temporarily unable to act on your behalf, the others may simply act alone, without any special documents or fuss. And you can name an alternate agent to take over if all of your agents must step down.

Allowing delegation in this situation could, in fact, create much unnecessary confusion. Because your agents may act independently, they could each delegate tasks to individuals that they choose—without consulting each other. When it comes to your finances, it's better not to open the door to that sort of chaos.

Estate tax savings. Some people with very substantial assets set up a gift-giving plan aimed at reducing the amount of property they leave at death—and so shrinking their eventual estate tax liability. If you have set up this sort of plan, you'll probably want to authorize your agent to continue it. (Your strategy may change, however, as estate tax law changes. For the latest, visit Nolo's website at www.nolo.com.)

Make sure your agent understands who should receive your property, how often, and in what amounts. You may want to explicitly limit the people and organizations to whom your agent may give gifts by listing them in your power of attorney document. (This is explained below.)

Gift Taxes

If your agent gives away more than a certain amount (currently $13,000) to any one person (except your spouse) or organization in one calendar year, a federal gift tax return will have to be filed. Gift tax may eventually have to be paid, but unless you give away or leave a very large amount of money, tax isn't usually paid until after your death. Making large gifts could put your agent in a bind. On one hand, your agent may feel that you would want to make a sizable gift—even if it's a taxable one—to a particular person or organization. On the other hand, making a taxable gift could increase the tax bill at your death.

For this reason, if you do permit your agent to make gifts, it's particularly important that you explain, ahead of time, what you intend, and what your limits are, if any.

Other gift-giving plans. You may want to donate regularly to your church or a favorite charity. Or perhaps you've made a commitment to help a family member with college or starting up a business. Allowing your agent to make gifts means that these plans can go forward.

But again, talk with your agent and give as much guidance as you can. Remember that you can use your form to name the specific people and organizations to whom your agent may give your money or property.

Loan Forgiveness

When you give your agent the power to make gifts, you also give the power to forgive (cancel) debts owed to you. If anyone owes you money and you've authorized your agent to make gifts to them, be sure you let your agent know how you feel about those debts. Must they be paid, or may your agent forgive them under some circumstances?

If you authorize gifts to your agent and he or she owes you money, your agent can forgive those debts, too. But for these debts to you, your agent can't cancel an amount worth more than his or her maximum gift amount in any calendar year. For example, say your son, whom you've named as agent, owes you $20,000. You've placed the annual gift limit at $7,000. He can forgive his debt to you at the rate of $7,000 per year.

Family emergencies. You may want your agent to be able to help out if a loved one is caught off guard by unexpected financial troubles. This is fine. But be sure your agent knows whom you'd want to help, what you consider an emergency, and what your limits are. Again, you may want to use your power of attorney form to limit the people to whom your agent can make gifts.

Gifts to the Agent

If you allow your agent to make gifts of your property, you must specifically decide whether or not your agent will be allowed to make gifts to himself or herself. This question raises some unique issues.

If you want to allow gifts to your agent, you must place an annual limit on those gifts. If you don't, *all* your property could be considered to legally belong to the agent if he or she dies before you do.

The sample clauses at the end of this section show you how to include the limit in your form. To avoid trouble with gift taxes, you may want to let the current gift tax threshold be your guide and set the limit at no more than $13,000. Whatever amount you choose, be sure it's far less than what you're worth. If you set the limit too high, you may in effect give everything to the agent.

Sample Clauses

Following are several sample clauses. You can include one of them in your form if you want to authorize your agent to make gifts of your property. Which one you should choose depends on who are the people you want to authorize to receive gifts, and on whether you want to name them in your form. Remember, any gifts your agent makes must be in your best interest.

> **Your Agent May Make Gifts to People Other Than Himself or Herself**
>
> My agent may make gifts of my property, including forgiveness of debts owed to me and completion of charitable pledges that I have made. However, my agent shall not (i) appoint, assign, or designate any of my assets, interests, or rights directly or indirectly to himself or herself, or his or her estate or creditors, or the creditors of his or her estate, (ii) disclaim assets to which I would otherwise be entitled if the effect of the disclaimer is to cause the assets to pass directly or indirectly to my agent or his or her estate, or (iii) use my assets to discharge any of his or her legal obligations, including any obligation of support owed to others, excluding me and those I am legally obligated to support.

> **Your Agent May Make Gifts to Recipients You List, but Not to Himself or Herself**
>
> My agent may make gifts of my property, including forgiveness of debts owed to me and completion of charitable pledges that I have made. However, the recipients of such gifts shall be limited to [*insert the names of people to whom your agent may make gifts, joined with "or"*].
>
> My agent shall not (i) appoint, assign, or designate any of my assets, interests, or rights directly or indirectly to himself or herself, or his or her estate or creditors, or the creditors of his or her estate, (ii) disclaim assets to which I would otherwise be entitled if the effect of the disclaimer is to cause such assets to pass directly or indirectly to my agent or his or her estate, or (iii) use my assets to discharge any of his or her legal obligations, including any obligation of support owed to others, excluding me and those I am legally obligated to support.

> **Your Agent May Make Gifts Only to Himself or Herself**
>
> Except as specified in this paragraph, my agent may not make gifts of my property or forgive debts owed to me. However, my agent may make gifts of my property to himself or herself as long as those gifts are not worth more than a total of $_____ in any calendar year.

> **Your Agent May Make Gifts to Anyone, Including Himself or Herself**
>
> My agent may make gifts of my property, including forgiveness of debts owed to me and completion of charitable pledges that I have made. However, my agent shall not make gifts of my property to himself or herself, or anyone he or she is legally obligated to support, worth more than a total of $_____ in any calendar year.

Your Agent May Make Gifts to Himself or Herself and to Other People You Name

My agent may make gifts of my property, including forgiveness of debts owed to me and completion of charitable pledges that I have made. However, the recipients of any such gifts shall be limited to _[insert the names of people to whom your agent may make gifts, joined with "or"]_ . My agent may also make gifts of my property to himself or herself, provided that any gifts to my agent, or anyone he or she is legally obligated to support, are not worth more than a total of $ _____ in any calendar year.

Your Agent May Make Gifts to Care for Your Pets

My agent may use my funds or other property as reasonably necessary to provide for the health, care, and welfare of any pets or animals that belong to me, including (but not limited to) expenditures for food, veterinary care, grooming, toys, day care, and temporary boarding or pet-sitting fees. I grant my agent the authority to maintain my pets or animals in the same standard of health, care, and welfare as I have done. For purposes of this document, any actions taken by my agent for the benefit of my pets or animals shall be considered taken for my own benefit.

Creating, Modifying, Revoking, or Funding a Trust

Although your agent is not allowed to make, modify, or revoke a will for you, you may grant your agent the power to set up, modify, or terminate a trust on your behalf. Including this power in your document allows your agent to do some planning that will permit your estate to avoid probate or estate taxes. You need not worry that your agent will go against your wishes and alter a plan you've already created for distributing your property after death—for example, by transferring assets you planned

to leave by will into a new living trust and designating new beneficiaries for those assets. California law forbids an agent from changing your beneficiaries unless you specifically grant such authority in your power of attorney document. (Cal. Prob. Code § 4264; *Schubert v. Reynolds*, 95 Cal.App.4th 100, 115 Cal.Rptr.2d 285 (2002).)

If you want to grant your agent only the power to set up and manage a trust for you, but not to change who will inherit your property, here's a clause that you can use:

My agent may create, modify, or revoke a trust on my behalf. If my agent creates a trust, my agent may designate or change trust beneficiaries but may not do so in a way that leaves property to different beneficiaries than those I have named in other estate planning documents.

On the other hand, if you want your agent to have the authority to change your beneficiaries, you can grant that broad power. If you want to give your agent this kind of control over your estate plan, it's very important that the two of you thoroughly discuss your wishes. And remember that your agent must always act in your best interests. Here is some language you can use to give broader powers to your agent:

My agent may create, modify, or revoke a trust on my behalf. If my agent creates a trust, my agent may designate or change trust beneficiaries even if doing so leaves property to different beneficiaries than those I have named in other estate planning documents.

If you use one of the clauses above to allow your agent to set up a trust for you, you'll also want to give your agent the power to fund that trust by transferring property to it. (If you granted the estate and trusts power discussed in "Granting Powers to Your Agent," above, your agent has the power to transfer items of your property into a revocable trust you've already created.) Here's the language to use:

> My agent may fund with my property a trust created by me or created for my benefit by my agent.

Finally, be aware that if, in your durable power, you grant the power to modify or revoke a trust, the trust instrument itself must also permit it. If you have existing trusts over which you wish to give your agent control, you may have to modify the trust documents to ensure your agent will have the necessary power.

Limits on the Agent's Authority

You can add your own restrictions or additions to the any of the powers you grant to your agent. For example, if a power listed on the form seems too broad, you can add limits to it. Here are a few examples.

Restricting the Sale of Your Home

Selling your home, especially if you've lived there many years, can be a disturbing prospect. You may not want your agent to sell your home—no matter what happens. If you've granted the real estate power, but you want to forbid your agent from selling or mortgaging your home, you can include a provision like the one below.

> My agent shall have no authority to sell, convey, exchange, transfer, or partition the real property, or any rights or security interest therein, of my principal place of residence, located at ___ [insert the full address of your home] ___ .

But think carefully before you tie the hands of your agent in this way. Of course you don't want to lose your home—but if a financial emergency makes it necessary, you may not want to leave your agent without options.

Especially if your spouse, domestic partner, or other co-owner of your home will be your agent, you probably want to trust that person to make a decision that's in your best interests.

Restrictions on Running a Small Business

If you have given your agent power over your small business interests but want to restrict the agent's freedom to sell or encumber the business, you can include a clause like this one:

> My agent shall have no authority to sell, transfer, or otherwise encumber my business, _[type the name and address of your business]_ .

If you don't want to include an outright ban on selling the business, you may still want someone else—your spouse or financial adviser, perhaps—to review and approve a sale. If that's the case, include a clause like this:

> If my agent deems it necessary to sell _[specify the property]_ , he or she shall do so only with the written approval of_ [insert the name and address of the person who must approve]_ .

Requiring the Approval of Others

You can require your agent to seek the approval of a trusted friend or family member before taking certain actions. If you wish to add this type of limitation to any power, you can use the following language:

> The agent's power to _[insert the power]_ may be exercised only upon written approval by _[insert the name and address of the person or people who must approve]_ .

Making Periodic Reports

Unless you require it, your agent doesn't have to report to anyone about your finances. Usually, that's fine. In some circumstances, though, you may want to require reports. For example, you may be able to defuse a potentially explosive personal conflict by reassuring mistrustful family members that they'll receive regular reports about your finances. You can use a clause like this one to require periodic reports to people that you name:

My agent shall prepare written _[quarterly, semi-annual, annual, or whatever period you choose]_ reports regarding my finances, including the income received and expenses incurred by my agent for me during the previous [_insert correct number of months depending on the period you choose_]. These reports shall be mailed within 30 days of each _[quarter, six-month period, year, or whatever period you choose]_ to _[insert the names and addresses of people to whom your agent must make reports]_ .

The idea of making your agent accountable to people may be appealing to you. But before you type up a long list of names of people to whom your agent must make reports, ask yourself whether these reports are truly necessary.

One of the most important reasons for making a power of attorney is to give control of your finances to someone you trust completely, bypassing the court system. One big advantage of this tactic is that you spare your agent the hassle and expense of preparing reports and accountings for a court.

If you want your agent to prepare reports so that someone can keep tabs on what he or she is doing, think again about the person you've named—and your level of trust.

Nominating a Conservator or Guardian

One last clause that you may want to include isn't really a special instruction to the agent, but it does concern the agent. It deals with what you want to happen in the highly unlikely event that

a court proceeding is ever brought to set aside or override your durable power of attorney. If your durable power of attorney is declared invalid, the court will appoint a conservator to handle your financial affairs.

To guard against the possibility that your plans for financial management might be thwarted if a court appoints a conservator, you can provide, in your durable power of attorney, that you want the person you choose as agent to be named as the conservator. Even if it's not required by law, most courts will honor your request absent a powerful reason not to.

Here's a clause you can include in the special instructions section of your form to nominate your agent as conservator or guardian:

If, in a court proceeding, it is ever resolved that I need a conservator, guardian, or other person to administer and supervise my estate, I nominate my agent to serve in that capacity. If my agent cannot serve, I nominate my alternate agent to serve.

If You Appointed More Than One Agent

If you named more than one agent, look for the heading in the form titled "EXERCISE OF POWER OF ATTORNEY WHERE MORE THAN ONE AGENT DESIGNATED." (If you named only one agent, skip to the next step.) Here, you must state whether or not you want to allow each agent to act separately (independently) on your behalf or whether they must all agree before taking action. (See "Appointing More Than One Person," above, for discussion of this issue.) You have two choices:

- To permit your agents to act independently, enter "separately" in the blank.
- To require your agents to act jointly, enter "jointly" in the blank.

Reliance by Third Parties

This clause tells a third party that it's safe to rely on the agent's authority when shown a copy of the durable power of attorney. (For a discussion of this issue, see "Will Your Power of Attorney Be Accepted?" above.)

Signing Your Durable Power of Attorney

You must sign the power of attorney in the presence of a notary public. Instructions are in "Making Your Durable Power of Attorney Legal," below.

Agent's Acceptance of Responsibility

This sentence at the end of the form means that if your agent exercises any authority under the power of attorney, he or she must act as your "fiduciary." A fiduciary must always act in your best interests. (For more information, see "Legal Responsibilities," above.)

Making Your Durable Power of Attorney Legal

After you've completed your durable power of attorney for finances, you must carry out a few simple tasks to make sure the document is legally valid. This section shows you what to do.

Before You Sign

Before you finalize your power of attorney, you may want to show it to the banks, brokers, insurers, and other financial institutions you expect your agent to deal with on your behalf.

Discussing your plans with people at these institutions now (and giving them a copy of the durable power of attorney after you sign it, if you wish), can make your agent's job easier. An institution may ask that you use its own form or

include specific language in your durable power of attorney, authorizing the agent to do certain things on your behalf. You may have to go along if you want cooperation later.

Making Your Document Legal

☐ Show the durable power of attorney to banks, brokers, insurers, and other financial institutions you expect your agent to deal with, to make sure they'll accept it.

☐ Sign the durable power of attorney in front of a notary public.

☐ Record (file) the durable power of attorney in the county land records office, if necessary.

☐ Distribute copies of the durable power of attorney to people the agent will deal with.

☐ Store the durable power of attorney where your agent will have quick access to it.

Sign and Notarize the Durable Power of Attorney

A durable power of attorney is a serious document, and to make it effective you must observe certain formalities when you sign it. Fortunately, these requirements aren't difficult to meet.

You must sign your durable power of attorney in the presence of a notary public for the state of California. California law requires this. (Cal. Prob. Code § 4402(c).)

The notary public watches you sign the durable power of attorney and then signs it too and stamps it with an official seal. The notary will want proof of your identity, such as a driver's license that bears your photo and signature. The notary's fee is usually just a few dollars—about $20 in most places.

Finding a notary public shouldn't be a problem; many advertise online. Or check with your bank, which may provide notarizations as a service to customers. Real estate offices and title companies also have notaries, as do many packaging stores.

Sample Durable Power of Attorney for Finances

Uniform Statutory Form Power of Attorney
California Probate Code Section 4401

NOTICE: THE POWERS GRANTED BY THIS DOCUMENT ARE BROAD AND SWEEPING. THEY ARE EXPLAINED IN THE UNIFORM STATUTORY FORM POWER OF ATTORNEY ACT (CALIFORNIA PROBATE CODE SECTIONS 4400–4465). THE POWERS LISTED IN THIS DOCUMENT DO NOT INCLUDE ALL POWERS THAT ARE AVAILABLE UNDER THE PROBATE CODE. ADDITIONAL POWERS AVAILABLE UNDER THE PROBATE CODE MAY BE ADDED BY SPECIFICALLY LISTING THEM UNDER THE SPECIAL INSTRUCTIONS SECTION OF THIS DOCUMENT. IF YOU HAVE ANY QUESTIONS ABOUT THESE POWERS, OBTAIN COMPETENT LEGAL ADVICE. THIS DOCUMENT DOES NOT AUTHORIZE ANYONE TO MAKE MEDICAL AND OTHER HEALTH CARE DECISIONS FOR YOU. YOU MAY REVOKE THIS POWER OF ATTORNEY IF YOU LATER WISH TO DO SO.

I _____ Lillian L. Woo, 8892 Grant St., Sacramento, CA 95822 _____ ,
Your Name and Address

appoint _____ Robert M. Woo, 8892 Grant St., Sacramento, CA 95822 _____ ,
Name and Address of the Person Appointed, or of Each Person Appointed If You Want to Designate More Than One

as my agent (attorney-in-fact) to act for me in any lawful way with respect to the following initialed subjects:

TO GRANT ALL OF THE FOLLOWING POWERS, INITIAL THE LINE IN FRONT OF (N) AND IGNORE THE LINES IN FRONT OF THE OTHER POWERS.

TO GRANT ONE OR MORE, BUT FEWER THAN ALL OF THE FOLLOWING POWERS, INITIAL THE LINE IN FRONT OF EACH POWER YOU ARE GRANTING.

TO WITHHOLD A POWER, DO NOT INITIAL THE LINE IN FRONT OF IT. YOU MAY, BUT NEED NOT, CROSS OUT EACH POWER WITHHELD.

INITIALS

_____ (A) Real property transactions.

_____ (B) Tangible personal property transactions.

_____ (C) Stock and bond transactions.

_____ (D) Commodity and option transactions.

_____ (E) Banking and other financial institution transactions.

_____ (F) Business operating transactions.

_____ (G) Insurance and annuity transactions.

_____ (H) Estate, trust, and other beneficiary transactions.

_____ (I) Claims and litigation.

_____ (J) Personal and family maintenance.

_____ (K) Benefits from Social Security, Medicare, Medicaid, or other governmental programs, or civil or military service.

_____ (L) Retirement plan transactions.

_____ (M) Tax matters.

LLW (N) ALL OF THE POWERS LISTED ABOVE.

YOU NEED NOT INITIAL ANY OTHER LINES IF YOU INITIAL LINE (N).

Sample Durable Power of Attorney for Finances (continued)

Special Instructions

ON THE FOLLOWING LINES YOU MAY GIVE SPECIAL INSTRUCTION LIMITING OR EXTENDING THE POWERS GRANTED TO YOUR AGENT.

If Robert M. Woo does not or ceases to serve as agent, I appoint Elaine P. Woo, 834 D St., Sacramento, CA, 95822 to serve as agent.

My agent may buy any assets of mine or engage in any transaction he or she deems in good faith to be in my interest, no matter what the interest or benefit to my agent.

My agent may commingle any of my funds with his or hers. However, if an alternate agent is serving under the document, the alternate may not commingle any of my funds with his or hers.

My agent may delegate, in writing, any authority granted under this power of attorney to a person he or she selects. Any such delegation shall state the period during which it's valid and specify the extent of the delegation.

UNLESS YOU DIRECT OTHERWISE ABOVE, THIS POWER OF ATTORNEY IS EFFECTIVE IMMEDIATELY AND WILL CONTINUE UNTIL IT IS REVOKED.

This power of attorney will continue to be effective even though I become incapacitated.

STRIKE THE PRECEDING SENTENCE IF YOU DO NOT WANT THIS POWER OF ATTORNEY TO CONTINUE IF YOU BECOME INCAPACITATED.

EXERCISE OF POWER OF ATTORNEY WHERE MORE THAN ONE AGENT DESIGNATED:

If I have designated more than one agent, the agents are to act _____ .

IF YOU APPOINTED MORE THAN ONE AGENT AND YOU WANT EACH AGENT TO BE ABLE TO ACT ALONE WITHOUT THE OTHER AGENT JOINING, WRITE THE WORD "SEPARATELY" IN THE BLANK SPACE ABOVE. IF YOU DO NOT INSERT ANY WORD IN THE BLANK SPACE, OR IF YOU INSERT THE WORD "JOINTLY," THEN ALL OF YOUR AGENTS MUST ACT OR SIGN TOGETHER.

Sample Durable Power of Attorney for Finances (continued)

I agree that any third party who receives a copy of this document may act under it. Revocation of the power of attorney is not effective as to a third party until the third party has actual knowledge of the revocation. I agree to indemnify the third party for any claims that arise against the third party because of reliance on this power of attorney.

Signed this ___16th___ day of ___September___, 20 _xx_

__Lillian L. Woo__
Your Signature

__343-54-1291__
Your Social Security Number

State of California, County of ___Sacramento___

BY ACCEPTING OR ACTING UNDER THE APPOINTMENT, THE AGENT ASSUMES THE FIDUCIARY AND OTHER LEGAL RESPONSIBILITIES OF AN AGENT.

Certificate of Acknowledgment of Notary Public

> A notary public or other officer completing this certificate verifies only the identity of the individual who signed the document to which this certificate is attached, and not the truthfulness, accuracy, or validity of that document.

State of California

County of ___Sacramento___ } ss

On ___September 16___, 20 _XX_, before me, ___Rose Livingston___, personally appeared ___Lillian L. Woo___, who proved to me on the basis of satisfactory evidence to be the person(s) whose name(s) is/are subscribed to the within instrument and acknowledged to me that he/she/they executed the same in his/her/their authorized capacity(ies), and that by his/her/their signature(s) on the instrument the person(s), or the entity upon behalf of which the person(s) acted, executed the instrument.

I certify under PENALTY OF PERJURY under the laws of the State of California that the foregoing paragraph is true and correct.

WITNESS my hand and official seal.

__Rose Livingston__
Notary Public for the State of California

[NOTARY SEAL]   My commission expires ___June 12, 20xx___

If you are gravely ill, you'll need to find a notary who will come to your home or hospital room. To arrange it, ask a hospital representative or call around to notaries listed online. Some hospitals provide notary services for free, but you can expect to pay a reasonable extra fee for a house call.

Putting Your Durable Power of Attorney on Public Record

You may need to put a copy of your durable power of attorney on file in the county recorder's office of any counties where you own real estate. The process of filing your document is called "recording."

When You Should Record Your Durable Power of Attorney

You must record the power of attorney only if it gives your agent authority over your real estate. Essentially, this means you must record the document if you granted the real estate power. In this case, if the document isn't in the public records, your agent won't be able to sell, mortgage, or transfer your real estate.

Recording makes it clear to all interested parties that the agent has power over the property. County land records are checked whenever real estate changes hands or is mortgaged; if your agent goes to sell or mortgage your real estate, there must be something in these public records that proves he or she has authority to do so.

There is no time limit on when you must record a durable power of attorney. If you don't expect your agent to act for you for many years (or ever), you may not want to record it immediately. Your agent can always record it later, if the document takes effect.

Even if recording is not legally required, you can go ahead and record your durable power of attorney; officials in some financial institutions may be reassured later on by seeing that you took that step.

Where to Record Your Power of Attorney

In California, each county has its own county recorder's office. Take the durable power of attorney to the local office in the county where your real estate is located. If you want your agent to have authority over real estate in more than one county, record the power of attorney in each county where you own property.

How to Record a Document

Recording a document is easy. You may even be able to do it by mail, but it's safer to go in person. The clerk will make a copy for the public record. It will be assigned a reference number, usually called an "instrument number." It will cost about $25 to record your document. If you have questions or need more information, most county recorder's offices have detailed websites. Search by your county's name and "recorder," for example, "Orange County recorder," or call the county recorder's office; you can find the number online or in the Government Listings section of the white pages under "Recorder" or "County Recorder."

What to Do With the Signed Document

The agent will need the original document to carry out your wishes.

If the power of attorney is to take effect immediately, give the original, signed and notarized document to the agent. If you named more than one agent, give the original document to one of them. Between them, they will have to work out the best way to prove their authority. For example, they may decide to visit some financial institutions or government offices together to establish themselves as your agents. Or they may need to take turns with the document. Some agencies, such as the IRS, will accept a copy of the document, rather than the original.

If the durable power of attorney won't become effective unless you become incapacitated (a springing durable power of attorney), keep the notarized, signed original yourself. Store it in a safe, convenient place to which the agent has quick access. A fireproof box in your home or office is fine. Just make sure the agent knows where it is.

A safe deposit box isn't the best place to store a springing durable power of attorney, unless the agent is a cotenant with access to the box. It's true that the power of attorney may give your agent the authority to open your safe deposit box, but if the document is locked in the box to begin with, the bank won't be able to confirm your agent's authority and your agent will be stuck. It's better just to keep the document wherever you file other important legal papers.

Making and Distributing Copies

If you wish, you can give copies of your document to the people your agent will need to deal with—banks or government offices, for example. If the durable power is already in their records, it may eliminate hassles for your agent later.

If you're making a springing durable power of attorney, however, it may seem premature to contact people and institutions about a document that may never go into effect. It's up to you.

Be sure to keep a list of everyone to whom you give a copy. If you later revoke your durable power of attorney, you must notify each institution of the revocation. (See below.)

Keeping Your Document Up to Date

If you make a springing durable power of attorney, it's a good idea to revoke it and create a new one every five to seven years, especially if your circumstances have changed significantly. A durable power of attorney never expires, but if the document was signed many years before it goes

into effect, the agent may have more difficulty getting banks, insurance companies, or people in government agencies to accept its authority.

Revoking a Durable Power of Attorney for Finances

After you make a power of attorney for finances, you can revoke it at any time, as long as you are of sound mind. Just carefully follow the procedure set out in this section.

Revoking a Durable Power of Attorney for Finances
☐ Prepare a notice of revocation.
☐ Sign the notice of revocation in front of a notary public.
☐ Record the notice of revocation at the county recorder's office, if necessary.
☐ Deliver a copy of the notice of revocation to the agent and each institution and person who has dealt or might deal with the former agent.

When to Revoke a Durable Power of Attorney for Finances

Here are the most common situations in which you should revoke a power of attorney and start fresh.

You want to change the terms of the power of attorney. There is no accepted way to amend a power of attorney. If you want to change your document—for example, to change the powers or to name a different agent—the safe course is to revoke the existing document and prepare a new one. Don't go back and modify your old document with pen or correction fluid—you could throw doubt on the authenticity of the whole thing.

SEE AN EXPERT

If your agent won't let go. An agent who refuses to accept a revocation can create serious problems. If you get into a dispute with your agent over whether or not your revocation is valid, consult a lawyer.

You move to another state. If you move to a new state, your agent may run into some trouble getting others to accept the validity of a power of attorney document signed in your former state. It's best to revoke your power of attorney and prepare a new document.

You lose the power of attorney document. If you conclude that you've really lost your signed power of attorney document, it's wise to formally revoke it, destroy any copies, and create a new one. Very few people are likely to accept your agent's authority if they can't look at the original document it's based on. By officially revoking the lost version, you minimize chances that it will cause confusion if it reappears someday.

You get married or divorced. If you get married after signing a power of attorney, you'll probably want to designate your new spouse to be your agent, if you named someone else originally.

As mentioned earlier, if you name your spouse or registered domestic partner as your agent and later part ways, you should revoke the power of attorney and create a new one, naming someone else as your agent.

Your agent becomes unavailable. If the person you named as your agent moves away, becomes ill, or is no longer closely involved with your life, you should appoint someone else to serve. To do that, revoke the old power of attorney and prepare a new one.

Your durable power of attorney is old. As discussed just above, if you make a springing durable power of attorney, it's a good idea to review it every five to seven years. If the document is signed many years before it goes into effect, the agent may have trouble getting others to accept it. You may want to revoke the document and make a new one.

How to Revoke a Durable Power of Attorney for Finances

Practically speaking, there are two ways to revoke your power of attorney for finances:

- by preparing and signing a document called a notice of revocation, or
- by telling your agent that his or her authority is revoked and destroying all copies of the power of attorney document.

The first method is preferable, because it creates proof that you really revoked the power of attorney. Here's how to proceed.

Step 1: Prepare a Notice of Revocation

The purpose of a notice of revocation is to notify your agent, and those he or she may have been dealing with, that you have revoked the durable power of attorney.

This book contains two kinds of notice of revocation forms for you to use. If you didn't record your power of attorney in the county land records office, use the standard form. If you did record the original power of attorney, you must also record the revocation; use the Notice of Revocation of Power of Attorney: Recorded. Sample forms follow; you can find the blank forms in Appendix B and as downloads from Nolo's website (see Appendix A for the link).

Step 2: Sign and Notarize the Revocation

You must sign and date the notice of revocation in front of a notary public. For information about finding a notary and getting your signature notarized, see "Sign and Notarize the Durable Power of Attorney," above.

Sample Notice of Revocation of Power of Attorney: Unrecorded

Notice of Revocation of Power of Attorney

I, _____ Ramona Ellsworth _____ ,

of the City of _____ Hornbrook _____ , County of _____ Siskiyou _____ ,

State of California, revoke the power of attorney dated _____ September 15, 20xx _____ ,

empowering _____ Bill Piersall _____

to act as my agent. I revoke and withdraw all power and authority granted under that power of attorney.

Dated: _____ February 5, 20xx _____

Ramona Ellsworth
Signature of Principal

_____ Ramona Ellsworth _____ , Principal

Certificate of Acknowledgment of Notary Public

> A notary public or other officer completing this certificate verifies only the identity of the individual who signed the document to which this certificate is attached, and not the truthfulness, accuracy, or validity of that document.

State of California

} ss

County of _____ Siskiyou _____

On _____ February 5 _____ , 20 __XX__ , before me, _____ Daniel Sweeny _____ ,
personally appeared _____ Ramona Ellsworth _____ , who
proved to me on the basis of satisfactory evidence to be the person(s) whose name(s) is/are subscribed to the within instrument and acknowledged to me that he/she/they executed the same in his/her/their authorized capacity(ies), and that by his/her/their signature(s) on the instrument the person(s), or the entity upon behalf of which the person(s) acted, executed the instrument.

I certify under PENALTY OF PERJURY under the laws of the State of California that the foregoing paragraph is true and correct.

WITNESS my hand and official seal.

Daniel Sweeny
Notary Public for the State of California

[NOTARY SEAL]   My commission expires _____ April 1, 20xx _____

Sample Notice of Revocation of Power of Attorney: Recorded

RECORDING REQUESTED BY
AND WHEN RECORDED MAIL TO

David L. Hernandez

45 N. Palm Drive

Blythe, CA 92225

Notice of Revocation of Power of Attorney

I, David L. Hernandez ,

of the City of Blythe , County of Riverside ,

State of California, revoke the power of attorney dated May 26, 20xx ,

empowering Francis M. Rowland

to act as my agent. I revoke and withdraw all power and authority granted under that power of attorney.

That power of attorney was recorded on May 30th , 20xx , with Instrument

Number 12345789 , in the Official Records, County of

Riverside , State of California.

Dated: November 2, 20xx

David L. Hernandez
Signature of Principal

David L. Hernandez , Principal

Certificate of Acknowledgment of Notary Public

A notary public or other officer completing this certificate verifies only the identity of the individual who signed the document to which this certificate is attached, and not the truthfulness, accuracy, or validity of that document.

State of California

County of Riverside   } ss

On November 2 , 20 xx , before me, Evelyn Kramer , personally appeared David L. Hernandez , who proved to me on the basis of satisfactory evidence to be the person(s) whose name(s) is/are subscribed to the within instrument and acknowledged to me that he/she/they executed the same in his/her/their authorized capacity(ies), and that by his/her/their signature(s) on the instrument the person(s), or the entity upon behalf of which the person(s) acted, executed the instrument.

I certify under PENALTY OF PERJURY under the laws of the State of California that the foregoing paragraph is true and correct.

WITNESS my hand and official seal.

Evelyn Kramer
Notary Public for the State of California

[NOTARY SEAL]   My commission expires August 1, 20xx

Step 3: Record the Notice of Revocation

If you recorded the original power of attorney at the county recorder's office, you must also record the revocation. How to record a document is explained in "Putting Your Durable Power of Attorney on Public Record," above.

But even if the original power of attorney was not recorded, you can record a revocation if you fear that the former agent might try to act without authorization. If the revocation is part of the public record, people who check those records (as anyone involved with real estate should) will know that the former agent is no longer authorized to act on your behalf.

Step 4: Notify Anyone Who Deals With the Former Agent

It's not enough to sign a revocation, or even to record it, for it to be properly effective; there's one more crucial step. You must send a copy of the notice of revocation to the former agent and all institutions and people who have dealt or might deal with the former agent.

If you don't give this written notification, people or institutions who don't know the power of attorney has been revoked might still enter into transactions with the former agent. If they do this in good faith, they are legally protected. (Cal. Prob. Code § 4151(b).) You could be held legally liable for the acts of your agent, even though you have revoked his or her authority. In other words, the legal burden is on you to be sure everyone knows you have revoked the power of attorney.

When you're ready to send out revocation notices, try to think of everyone with whom the agent may have had dealings. Here are some examples:

- banks
- mortgage companies
- title companies
- stockbrokers
- insurance companies
- credit card companies
- Social Security offices
- Medicare or Medicaid offices
- IRS
- pension fund administrators
- post offices
- hospitals
- doctors
- schools
- relatives
- business partners
- landlords
- lawyers
- accountants
- real estate agents, and
- maintenance and repair people.

Help Beyond the Book

Legal Document Assistants..108

Lawyers...108

    Looking for a Lawyer...108

    Working With a Lawyer...109

    Lawyers' Fees...109

Getting More Information on Your Own...109

    Online Legal Research..110

    Going to a Law Library..110

When you prepare your own advance health care directive and durable power of attorney for finances with this book, you probably won't need to see a lawyer. If, however, you have specific questions or unusual circumstances—for example, the potential for family squabbles, worries about your agent's powers, or a very large amount of property—you may benefit from legal advice.

If you do need more legal information or advice, you can talk to a lawyer or look for the answers yourself, by searching for information online or going to the law library. If you just want clerical help typing or recording your document, you may want to get help from a legal document assistant.

Legal Document Assistants

Even if you need "legal" help, you may not need a lawyer. People who operate document preparation services, usually called "legal document assistants" or LDAs, are experts at typing up legal documents. They are not lawyers and do not give legal advice, but if you know what you want, a document preparer can help you complete legal paperwork at an affordable price. For example, if you need to retype one of the forms in this book—say you need more room for special instructions in your durable power of attorney for finances or you want to remove optional parts of your advance health care directive—and you're concerned about getting everything in the right place, a document assistant can probably help.

Here are some things to look for when choosing a document preparer.

An established or recommended service. Few document assistants stay in business unless they provide honest and competent services. A service recommended by a social service agency, friend, court clerk, or lawyer is probably a good place to take your business.

Reasonable fees. California document assistants will probably charge between $100 and $300 to type up your documents, depending on where you live and the complexity of your forms.

Trained staff. One indication of whether or not people are committed to providing good services is if they have undertaken skills training through legal document assistant associations and continuing education seminars.

Lawyers

Lawyers are costly. Estate planning fees usually range from $200 to $500 per hour. But if your situation is complex and you want professional help, a good estate planning specialist can be well worth the cost.

Looking for a Lawyer

Ideally, you'll find an attorney with whom you have personal rapport and who treats you as an equal. Here are some suggestions to help you find a lawyer you'll like.

Family, friends, and acquaintances. When looking for a good lawyer, especially an estate planning expert, personal contacts are the traditional, and probably the best, method. If a relative or friend who has good business and financial sense recommends an estate planning lawyer, chances are you'll like the lawyer, too. If nothing turns up, check with people you know in any business, political, or social organization with which you're involved. Assuming they themselves have good sense, they may well be able to point you to a competent lawyer who handles estate planning matters and whose point of view is similar to yours.

Other lawyers. Another good approach is to ask for help from a lawyer you know and like personally, but who works in another legal field. Very likely the lawyer you know can refer you to a trustworthy estate planning expert.

Nolo's Lawyer Directory. At www.nolo.com/ lawyers, Nolo offers a directory that provides detailed profiles of attorneys with information to help you select the right lawyer. Lawyers use their profiles to describe their experience, education, and fees and also to tell you something about the lawyer's general approach to practicing law. For example, each lawyer states whether he or she is willing to review documents or coach clients who are doing their own legal work.

Attorney referral services. Your local bar association may have an attorney referral service, which differs from a directory in that a referral service will gather some information about your legal needs and match you with attorneys who might be a good fit for you. Usually, you'll get only a few names of attorneys to consider, chosen for you by the people running the referral service, rather than having the entire directory to choose from on your own. It may be possible to find a skilled attorney through a referral service, but be sure to ask the attorney about his or her credentials and experience.

Working With a Lawyer

Before you talk to a lawyer, try to decide what kind of help you really need. Do you want someone to review your documents to make sure they look all right? Or do you want advice on a complete estate plan? If you don't clearly tell the lawyer what you want, you may find yourself agreeing to more than you'd planned.

Before you see a lawyer, a good strategy is to write down your questions as specifically as you can. If the lawyer doesn't give you clear, concise answers, say thank you and try someone else. Preparing a valid durable power of attorney for finances and health care directive isn't an overly complicated job in most cases; a knowledgeable lawyer should be able to give you satisfactory answers on the spot.

If the lawyer says little except to ask that matters be placed in his or her hands—for a substantial fee, of course—watch out. You're either dealing with someone who doesn't know the answer and won't admit it or someone who doesn't want to treat you as an equal. You deserve better.

Lawyers' Fees

Fees for estate planning lawyers can be steep—commonly hundreds of dollars an hour. Some lawyers also offer to prepare a standard estate plan, usually consisting of a will, advance directive, and powers of attorney, for a flat fee. That arrangement can work well, because you don't have to worry about the bill going up every time you have a question for the lawyer.

No matter how much you like your lawyer, be sure to settle your fee arrangement—in writing—at the start of your relationship. In addition to the amount charged per hour, it's also prudent to get an estimate of how many hours your lawyer expects to spend on the work.

Getting More Information on Your Own

As you prepare your documents, you may find yourself wanting to know more about a particular aspect of the law. For instance, you may want to look up some of the California Probate Code sections that are listed in this book, to learn more details about a particular matter or just to read the law itself.

Fortunately, the laws governing medical directives and powers of attorney are not particularly difficult to research.

California Probate Code	
Advance health care directives	Sections 4600–4948
DNR orders	Sections 4780–4786
Durable powers of attorney for finances	Sections 4000–4545
Conservatorship proceedings	Sections 1800–2955

Online Legal Research

The fastest way to find the information you need is to use your computer. You can look up any section of the California Probate Code online by visiting Nolo's legal research center at www.nolo.com/legal-research/state-law.html. Once there, choose "California" and then make your way to the "California Code," which is the collection of California statutes. You can look up a specific Probate Code section by number or search for statutes that contain particular words.

Be warned that statutes are rarely easy to read. Commonly, they are written in dense prose, full of incredibly long sentences, obscure legal terms, and cross-references to other statutes. Wade through them as best you can, and expect to read any section you're interested in several times. Take comfort—most lawyers have to do the same.

You can also browse Nolo's website for lots of other helpful legal information and links.

Going to a Law Library

There are several kinds of law libraries available to you:

- a public law library (usually located in or near the county courthouse)
- a public library with a good law collection, or
- a library at a public (or even private, if you ask permission) law school.

When you get to the library, you'll need the help of a kind reference librarian to point you in the right direction. Law librarians are almost always helpful and courteous to nonlawyers who undertake their own legal research.

The California Probate Code. The first thing to do is ask the librarian where to find the California Probate Code. This is where you're going to find most of the laws that govern estate planning and planning for incapacity in California. If you can, get an "annotated version," which contains both the state statutes and excerpts from any relevant court cases and references to related articles.

Once you've found the Probate Code, you can look up the laws that govern medical directives and powers of attorney. The laws you want will be grouped together in a few different areas of the code.

When you find what you're looking for, make sure you're reading the most recent version of the statute by checking the back of the statute book to see if there's a supplement (called a "pocket part") inserted inside the back cover. Pocket parts contain statutory changes (and summaries of related court decisions) made since the hardback book was printed.

After you've looked at the basic law, you'll probably want to check any recent court decisions mentioned in the "Annotation" section of the code that immediately follows the law itself.

Form books. Form books, which are how-to-do-it books written primarily for lawyers, can also be helpful. In particular, you should ask the law librarian to point you to *California Durable Powers of Attorney* from Continuing Education of the Bar (CEB), which is a very comprehensive and not-too-convoluted lawyer's guide to helping clients plan for incapacity. This form book comes in a big binder, and it delves more deeply into some of the issues we've discussed in earlier chapters, including drafting specific clauses for complicated health care or financial situations and determining mental capacity.

 RESOURCE

More help finding the law. *Legal Research: How to Find & Understand the Law,* by Stephen Elias and the editors of Nolo, is a hands-on guide to researching legal issues. It addresses research methods in detail and should answer most questions that arise in the course of your research. In particular, it contains a good discussion of how to read and analyze statutes, and instructions for looking up court cases.

How to Use the Downloadable Forms on Nolo.com

Editing RTFs: General Instructions 112

Downloadable Files 113

You can download interactive versions of the forms in this book at: **www.nolo.com/back-of-book/CPOA.html** Several types of files come with this book:

- **RTFs.** Most of the forms in this book are RTF files. You can open, edit, print, and save these form files with most word processing programs, such as Microsoft's *Word*, Corel's *WordPerfect*, or Apple's *Pages*.

CAUTION
It's crucial that you open the download-able RTF files with your word processing program. If you click on them and they open directly in a simple text editing program, some of the legally required formatting in your forms may be lost. Before you begin working on your forms, double check that you are working in your word processing program.

- **PDFs.** You can view these files with Adobe *Reader*, free software from www.adobe. com. PDFs are designed to be printed out and completed by hand.
- **MP3s.** You can listen to a discussion of living wills and medical directives on your computer. Most computers come with a media player that plays MP3 files, or you may have installed one on your own.

Editing RTFs: General Instructions

When you edit RTF forms in your word processing program, refer to the book's instructions and sample forms for help about what should go in each blank.

- **Underlines.** Underlines indicate where to enter information. After filling in the needed text, delete the underline. In most word processing programs you can do this by highlighting the underlined portion and typing CTRL+U.
- **Bracketed and italicized text.** Bracketed and italicized text indicates instructions. Be sure to remove all instructional text before you finalize your document.
- **Optional text.** Optional text gives you the choice to include or exclude text. Delete any optional text you don't want to use. Renumber numbered items, if necessary.
- **Alternative text.** Alternative text gives you the choice between two or more text options. Delete those options you don't want to use. Renumber numbered items, if necessary.
- **Signature lines.** Signature lines should appear on a page with at least some text from the document itself.

If you need help using your word processing program, please refer to your software's help documents. We're sorry, but Nolo cannot answer questions about how to use your computer or your software.

CAUTION
In accordance with U.S. copyright laws, the forms provided by this book are for your personal use only.

Downloadable Files

The following files are in RTF format:

Form Title	File Name
Advance Health Care Directive	HealthCareDir.rtf
Revocation of Advance Health Care Directive	HealthDirRevoc.rtf
Uniform Statutory Form Power of Attorney	PowAttorney.rtf
Authorization for Disclosure and Use of Protected Health Information	HIPAARelease.rtf
Physician's Determination of Incapacity	Incapacity.rtf
Revocation of Durable Power of Attorney for Finances: Recorded	RecPowRevoc.rtf
Revocation of Durable Power of Attorney for Finances: Unrecorded	UnrecPowRevoc.rtf

The following files are in PDF format:

Title	File Name
Wallet Medical Emergency Card	WalletCard.pdf
Making Final Arrangements	Arrangements.pdf

The following is an audio file in MP3 format:

Title	File Name
Living Wills and Medical Directives	70LivingWill.mp3

Forms

Name of Form	Chapter in Book
Advance Health Care Directive	2
Wallet Medical Emergency Card	2
Revocation of Advance Health Care Directive	2
Uniform Statutory Form Power of Attorney	4
Authorization for Disclosure and Use of Protected Health Information (HIPAA Release)	4
Physician's Determination of Incapacity	4
Revocation of Durable Power of Attorney for Finances: Recorded	4
Revocation of Durable Power of Attorney for Finances: Unrecorded	4

Advance Health Care Directive

Explanation

You have the right to give instructions about your own health care. You also have the right to name someone else to make health care decisions for you. This form lets you do either or both of these things. It also lets you express your wishes regarding donation of organs and the designation of your primary physician. If you use this form, you may complete or modify all or any part of it. You are free to use a different form.

Part 1 of this form is a power of attorney for health care. Part 1 lets you name another individual as agent to make health care decisions for you if you become incapable of making your own decisions or if you want someone else to make those decisions for you now even though you are still capable. You may also name an alternate agent to act for you if your first choice is not willing, able, or reasonably available to make decisions for you. (Your agent may not be an operator or employee of a community care facility or a residential care facility where you are receiving care, or your supervising health care provider or employee of the health care institution where you are receiving care, unless your agent is related to you, is your registered domestic partner, or is a coworker.)

Unless the form you sign limits the authority of your agent, your agent may make all health care decisions for you. This form has a place for you to limit the authority of your agent. You need not limit the authority of your agent if you wish to rely on your agent for all health care decisions that may have to be made. If you choose not to limit the authority of your agent, your agent will have the right to:

- Consent or refuse consent to any care, treatment, service, or procedure to maintain, diagnose, or otherwise affect a physical or mental condition.
- Select or discharge health care providers and institutions.
- Approve or disapprove diagnostic tests, surgical procedures, and programs of medication.
- Direct the provision, withholding, or withdrawal of artificial nutrition and hydration and all other forms of health care, including cardiopulmonary resuscitation.
- Make anatomical gifts, authorize an autopsy, and direct disposition of remains.

Part 2 of this form lets you give specific instructions about any aspect of your health care, whether or not you appoint an agent. Choices are provided for you to express your wishes regarding the provision, withholding, or withdrawal of treatment to keep you alive, as well as the provision of pain relief. Space is also provided for you to add to the choices you have made or for you to write out any additional wishes. If you are satisfied to allow your agent to determine what is best for you in making end-of-life decisions, you need not fill out Part 2 of this form.

Part 3 of this form lets you express an intention to donate your bodily organs and tissues following your death. Part 4 of this form lets you designate a physician to have primary responsibility for your health care.

After completing this form, sign and date the form at the end. The form must be signed by two qualified witnesses or acknowledged before a notary public. Give a copy of the signed and completed form to your physician, to any other health care providers you may have, to any health care institution at which you are receiving care, and to any health care agents you have named. You should talk to the person you have named as agent to make sure that he or she understands your wishes and is willing to take the responsibility. You have the right to revoke this advance health care directive or replace this form at any time.

Part 1: Power of Attorney for Health Care

1. **Designation of Agent: I,** _____ , of

    _____ ,

    California, designate the following individual as my agent to make health care decisions for me:

    _____
    Name of Individual You Choose as Agent

    _____
    Address

    _____   _____   _____
    City   State   Zip Code

    _____   _____
    Home Phone   Work Phone

    First Alternate Agent (Optional): If I revoke my agent's authority or if my agent is not willing, able, or reasonably available to make a health care decision for me, I designate as my first alternate agent:

    _____
    Name of Individual You Choose as First Alternate Agent

    _____
    Address

    _____   _____   _____
    City   State   Zip Code

    _____   _____
    Home Phone   Work Phone

    Second Alternate Agent (Optional): If I revoke the authority of my agent and first alternate agent or if neither is willing, able, or reasonably available to make a health care decision for me, I designate as my second alternate agent:

    _____
    Name of Individual You Choose as Second Alternate Agent

    _____
    Address

    _____   _____   _____
    City   State   Zip Code

    _____   _____
    Home Phone   Work Phone

2. **Agent's Authority:** My agent is authorized to make all health care decisions for me, including decisions to provide, withhold, or withdraw artificial nutrition and hydration and all other forms of health care to keep me alive, except as I state here:

    _____

    _____

    _____

    _____

    _____

    _____

    _____

    Add additional sheets if needed

3. **When Agent's Authority Becomes Effective:** My agent's authority becomes effective when my primary physician determines that I am unable to make my own health care decisions unless I mark the following box. If I mark this box ☐ , my agent's authority to make health care decisions for me takes effect immediately.

4. **Agent's Obligation:** My agent shall make health care decisions for me in accordance with this power of attorney for health care, any instructions I give in Part 2 of this form, and my other wishes to the extent known to my agent. To the extent my wishes are unknown, my agent shall make health care decisions for me in accordance with what my agent determines to be in my best interest. In determining my best interest, my agent shall consider my personal values to the extent known to my agent.

5. **Agent's Postdeath Authority:** My agent is authorized to make anatomical gifts, authorize an autopsy, and direct disposition of my remains, except as I state here or in Part 3 of this form:

_____

_____

_____

_____

_____

_____

_____

_____

_____

_____

_____

_____

_____

_____

_____

_____

_____

Add additional sheets if needed

6. **Nomination of Conservator:** If a conservator of my person needs to be appointed for me by a court, I nominate the agent designated in this form. If that agent is not willing, able, or reasonably available to act as conservator, I nominate the alternate agents whom I have named, in the order designated.

Part 2: Instructions for Health Care

(If you fill out this part of the form, you may strike any wording you do not want.)

7. **End-of-Life Decisions:** I direct that my health care providers and others involved in my care provide, withhold, or withdraw treatment in accordance with the choice I have marked below:

☐ **a. Choice Not to Prolong Life**
I do not want my life to be prolonged if (1) I have an incurable and irreversible condition that will result in my death within a relatively short time, (2) I become unconscious and, to a reasonable degree of medical certainty, I will not regain consciousness, or (3) the likely risks and burdens of treatment would outweigh the expected benefits.

☐ **b. Choice to Prolong Life**

I want my life to be prolonged as long as possible within the limits of generally accepted health care standards.

8. **Relief From Pain:** Except as I state in the following space, I direct that treatment for alleviation of pain or discomfort be provided at all times, even if it hastens my death:

_____

_____

_____

_____

_____

_____

_____

_____

Add additional sheets if needed

9. **Other Wishes:** (*If you do not agree with any of the optional choices above and wish to write your own, or if you wish to add to the instructions you have given above, you may do so here.*) I direct that:

_____

_____

_____

_____

_____

_____

_____

_____

_____

Add additional sheets if needed

Part 3: Donation of Organs at Death

10. **Wishes for Organ Donation:** Upon my death (*mark applicable box*):

☐ **a. I give any needed organs, tissues, or parts.**

☐ **b. I give the following organs, tissues, or parts only:**

_____

_____

_____

_____

_____

_____

_____

Add additional sheets if needed

☐ **c. My gift is for the following purposes** (*strike any of the following you do not want*):

    1. Transplant

    2. Therapy

    3. Research

    4. Education

Part 4: Primary Physician

11. **Designation of Primary Physician:** I designate the following physician as my primary physician:

_____
Name of Physician

_____
Address

_____
City   State   Zip Code

_____
Phone

Secondary Designation: If the physician I have designated above is not willing, able, or reasonably available to act as my primary physician, I designate the following physician as my primary physician:

_____
Name of Physician

_____
Address

_____
City   State   Zip Code

_____
Phone

Part 5: Signatures

12. **Effect of Copy:** A copy of this form has the same effect as the original.

13. **Signature:** Sign and date the form here:

Dated: _____

_____
Your Signature

_____
Print Your Name

Alternative #1: Witnesses

14. **Statement of Witnesses:** I declare under penalty of perjury under the laws of California (1) that the individual who signed or acknowledged this advance health care directive is personally known to me, or that the individual's identity was proven to me by convincing evidence, (2) that the individual signed or acknowledged this advance directive in my presence, (3) that the individual appears to be of sound mind and under no duress, fraud, or undue influence, (4) that I am not a person appointed as agent by this advance directive, and (5) that I am not the individual's health care provider, an employee of the individual's health care provider, the operator of a community care facility, an employee of an operator of a community care facility, the operator of a residential care facility for the elderly, nor an employee of an operator of a residential care facility for the elderly.

First Witness

_____
Signature of Witness

_____
Print Name

_____
Address

_____
Date

Second Witness

_____
Signature of Witness

_____
Print Name

_____
Address

_____
Date

15. **Additional Statement of Witnesses:** (*One of the above witnesses must also sign the following declaration.*)

    I further declare under penalty of perjury under the laws of California that I am not related to the individual executing this advance health care directive by blood, marriage, or adoption, and to the best of my knowledge, I am not entitled to any part of the individual's estate upon his or her death under a will now existing or by operation of law.

_____
Signature of Witness

Alternative #2: Notarization

Certificate of Acknowledgment of Notary Public

> A notary public or other officer completing this certificate verifies only the identity of the individual who signed the document to which this certificate is attached, and not the truthfulness, accuracy, or validity of that document.

State of California

County of _____ } ss

On _____ , _____ , before me, _____ ,

personally appeared _____ , who proved to me on the basis of satisfactory evidence to be the person(s) whose name(s) is/are subscribed to the within instrument and acknowledged to me that he/she/they executed the same in his/her/their authorized capacity(ies), and that by his/her/their signature(s) on the instrument the person(s), or the entity upon behalf of which the person(s) acted, executed the instrument.

I certify under PENALTY OF PERJURY under the laws of the State of California that the foregoing paragraph is true and correct.

WITNESS my hand and official seal.

_____
Notary Public for the State of California

[NOTARY SEAL]   My commission expires _____

16. **SPECIAL WITNESS REQUIREMENT:** (*The following statement is required only if you are a patient in a skilled nursing facility—a health care facility that provides skilled nursing care and supportive care to patients whose primary need is for availability of skilled nursing care on an extended basis. The patient advocate or ombudsman must sign the following statement.*)

Statement of Patient Advocate or Ombudsman

I declare under penalty of perjury under the laws of California that I am a patient advocate or ombudsman as designated by the State Department of Aging and that I am serving as a witness as required by Section 4675 of the Probate Code.

_____
Signature of Patient Advocate or Ombudsman

_____
Print Name

_____
Address

_____
Date

Cut →

Attention: Emergency Medical Personnel

I, _____ ,

[insert your name] of _____

_____ [insert your address]

have prepared an advance health care directive stating the type
of medical care I wish to receive if I am incapacitated and unable
to speak for myself. I have also appointed a health care agent to
oversee my wishes. In the event of a medical emergency, please
contact one of the people listed on the reverse of this card, in the
order listed.

©Nolo 2016   [OVER]

Fold →

_____
[insert the location of an easy-to-find copy of your directive]

My advance directive for health care is located:
_____

[insert your doctor's name and phone number]

My Primary Physician:
_____

_____
My Alternate Agent:

[insert agent's name
and phone numbers where agent can be reached in an emergency]

_____
[insert agent's name

_____
My Agent:

Revocation of Advance Health Care Directive

I, _____ ,

of the City of _____ , County of _____ ,

State of California, revoke the advance health care directive dated _____ ,

empowering _____

to make health care decisions for me. I revoke and withdraw all power and authority granted under that

directive.

Dated: _____

_____

Signature of Principal

_____

Print Principal's Name

Uniform Statutory Form Power of Attorney
California Probate Code Section 4401

NOTICE: THE POWERS GRANTED BY THIS DOCUMENT ARE BROAD AND SWEEPING. THEY ARE EXPLAINED IN THE UNIFORM STATUTORY FORM POWER OF ATTORNEY ACT (CALIFORNIA PROBATE CODE SECTIONS 4400–4465). THE POWERS LISTED IN THIS DOCUMENT DO NOT INCLUDE ALL POWERS THAT ARE AVAILABLE UNDER THE PROBATE CODE. ADDITIONAL POWERS AVAILABLE UNDER THE PROBATE CODE MAY BE ADDED BY SPECIFICALLY LISTING THEM UNDER THE SPECIAL INSTRUCTIONS SECTION OF THIS DOCUMENT. IF YOU HAVE ANY QUESTIONS ABOUT THESE POWERS, OBTAIN COMPETENT LEGAL ADVICE. THIS DOCUMENT DOES NOT AUTHORIZE ANYONE TO MAKE MEDICAL AND OTHER HEALTH CARE DECISIONS FOR YOU. YOU MAY REVOKE THIS POWER OF ATTORNEY IF YOU LATER WISH TO DO SO.

I _____ ,
Your Name and Address

appoint _____ ,
Name and Address of the Person Appointed, or of Each Person Appointed If You Want to Designate More Than One

as my agent (attorney-in-fact) to act for me in any lawful way with respect to the following initialed subjects:

TO GRANT ALL OF THE FOLLOWING POWERS, INITIAL THE LINE IN FRONT OF (N) AND IGNORE THE LINES IN FRONT OF THE OTHER POWERS.

TO GRANT ONE OR MORE, BUT FEWER THAN ALL OF THE FOLLOWING POWERS, INITIAL THE LINE IN FRONT OF EACH POWER YOU ARE GRANTING.

TO WITHHOLD A POWER, DO NOT INITIAL THE LINE IN FRONT OF IT. YOU MAY, BUT NEED NOT, CROSS OUT EACH POWER WITHHELD.

INITIALS

_____ (A) Real property transactions.

_____ (B) Tangible personal property transactions.

_____ (C) Stock and bond transactions.

_____ (D) Commodity and option transactions.

_____ (E) Banking and other financial institution transactions.

_____ (F) Business operating transactions.

_____ (G) Insurance and annuity transactions.

_____ (H) Estate, trust, and other beneficiary transactions.

_____ (I) Claims and litigation.

_____ (J) Personal and family maintenance.

_____ (K) Benefits from Social Security, Medicare, Medicaid, or other governmental programs, or civil or military service.

_____ (L) Retirement plan transactions.

_____ (M) Tax matters.

_____ (N) ALL OF THE POWERS LISTED ABOVE.

YOU NEED NOT INITIAL ANY OTHER LINES IF YOU INITIAL LINE (N).

Special Instructions

ON THE FOLLOWING LINES YOU MAY GIVE SPECIAL INSTRUCTION LIMITING OR EXTENDING THE POWERS GRANTED TO YOUR AGENT.

_____

_____

_____

_____

_____

_____

_____

_____

_____

_____

_____

_____

_____

_____

_____

_____

UNLESS YOU DIRECT OTHERWISE ABOVE, THIS POWER OF ATTORNEY IS EFFECTIVE IMMEDIATELY AND WILL CONTINUE UNTIL IT IS REVOKED.

This power of attorney will continue to be effective even though I become incapacitated.

STRIKE THE PRECEDING SENTENCE IF YOU DO NOT WANT THIS POWER OF ATTORNEY TO CONTINUE IF YOU BECOME INCAPACITATED.

EXERCISE OF POWER OF ATTORNEY WHERE MORE THAN ONE AGENT DESIGNATED:

If I have designated more than one agent, the agents are to act _____ .

IF YOU APPOINTED MORE THAN ONE AGENT AND YOU WANT EACH AGENT TO BE ABLE TO ACT ALONE WITHOUT THE OTHER AGENT JOINING, WRITE THE WORD "SEPARATELY" IN THE BLANK SPACE ABOVE. IF YOU DO NOT INSERT ANY WORD IN THE BLANK SPACE, OR IF YOU INSERT THE WORD "JOINTLY," THEN ALL OF YOUR AGENTS MUST ACT OR SIGN TOGETHER.

I agree that any third party who receives a copy of this document may act under it. Revocation of the power of attorney is not effective as to a third party until the third party has actual knowledge of the revocation. I agree to indemnify the third party for any claims that arise against the third party because of reliance on this power of attorney.

Signed this _____ day of _____ , 20_____

_____
Your Signature

_____
Your Social Security Number

State of California, County of _____

BY ACCEPTING OR ACTING UNDER THE APPOINTMENT, THE AGENT ASSUMES THE FIDUCIARY AND OTHER LEGAL RESPONSIBILITIES OF AN AGENT.

Certificate of Acknowledgment of Notary Public

A notary public or other officer completing this certificate verifies only the identity of the individual who signed the document to which this certificate is attached, and not the truthfulness, accuracy, or validity of that document.

State of California

County of _____   } ss

On _____ , 20_____ , before me, _____ ,
personally appeared _____ , who proved to me on the basis of satisfactory evidence to be the person(s) whose name(s) is/are subscribed to the within instrument and acknowledged to me that he/she/they executed the same in his/her/their authorized capacity(ies), and that by his/her/their signature(s) on the instrument the person(s), or the entity upon behalf of which the person(s) acted, executed the instrument.

I certify under PENALTY OF PERJURY under the laws of the State of California that the foregoing paragraph is true and correct.

WITNESS my hand and official seal.

_____
Notary Public for the State of California

[NOTARY SEAL]   My commission expires _____

Authorization for Disclosure and Use of Protected Health Information

Authorization. I, _____ ,
hereby authorize the disclosure and release of any of my individually identifiable
health information and any other medical records ("my medical records") to the
following person(s) who has or have been designated by me to act as my agent,
attorney-in-fact, successor trustee, or other personal representative, hereafter
referred to individually or collectively as "my agent."

Name of Agent	Address	Telephone
Name of Agent	Address	Telephone
Name of Agent	Address	Telephone

Purpose. This authorization is for the purpose of enabling my agent to carry
out the agent's duties toward me, as determined by my agent, including (but
not limited to) making a determination as to my incapacity for purposes of
establishing my agent's authority to act on my behalf. I intend that my agent shall
be treated as I would be regarding the use and disclosure of my medical records.

Persons authorized. The persons or entities who are authorized to disclose and
release my medical records to my agent are my treating physicians and any other
person, entity, or entities who is or are in possession of my medical records and
subject to the privacy requirements of the Health Insurance Portability and
Accountability Act of 1996 (HIPAA), 42 U.S.C. Section 1320d and 45 CFR parts
160, 164, or any successor legislation, and the California Confidentiality of Medical
Information Act, Civil Code Sections 56 to 56.37, or any successor legislation.

Effective date and duration. This authorization is effective immediately. It
will remain in effect until one year after my death, unless terminated earlier by
operation of law or revoked by me.

Right to revoke. I understand that I may revoke this authorization at any time by
signing a written statement of revocation and delivering it to any person acting as
my agent or to any physician or entity holding my protected health information. I
also understand that any such revocation will not be effective with regard to any
protected health information released to my agent by any person acting in good-
faith reliance on this authorization without actual knowledge of the revocation.

No conditions imposed. I understand that a person or entity covered by this
authorization may in limited circumstances legally condition treatment, payment,
enrollment, or eligibility for benefits on whether I sign an authorization. I am

signing this authorization for the purpose of planning for incapacity and not as a condition imposed by any person or entity.

Redisclosure of information. My agent may not redisclose my protected health care information except as required or permitted by law. I understand that any information redisclosed by my agent may no longer be protected by HIPAA regulations.

Release from liability. I release any person relying on this authorization from any liability arising from the release of my medical records to my agent in reliance on this authorization while it is in effect.

Copies. A copy of this authorization may be used in place and instead of the original.

Date: _____

Signature: _____

Printed Name: _____

Certificate of Acknowledgment of Notary Public

A notary public or other officer completing this certificate verifies only the identity of the individual who signed the document to which this certificate is attached, and not the truthfulness, accuracy, or validity of that document.

State of California

County of _____ } ss

On _____, 20_____ , before me, _____ , personally appeared _____ , who proved to me on the basis of satisfactory evidence to be the person(s) whose name(s) is/are subscribed to the within instrument and acknowledged to me that he/she/they executed the same in his/her/their authorized capacity(ies), and that by his/her/their signature(s) on the instrument the person(s), or the entity upon behalf of which the person(s) acted, executed the instrument.

I certify under PENALTY OF PERJURY under the laws of the State of California that the foregoing paragraph is true and correct.

WITNESS my hand and official seal.

_____
Notary Public for the State of California

[NOTARY SEAL]   My commission expires _____

Physician's Determination of Incapacity

I, _____ ,

of the City of _____ , County of _____ ,

State of California, declare under penalty of perjury that:

1. I am a physician licensed to practice in the state of California.

2. I examined _____

    on _____ , _____ . It is my professional opinion that

    _____

    is currently incapacitated and unable to manage his/her finances and property.

Dated: _____

_____
Signature of Physician

_____ , Physician

Certificate of Acknowledgment of Notary Public

> A notary public or other officer completing this certificate verifies only the identity of the individual who signed the document to which this certificate is attached, and not the truthfulness, accuracy, or validity of that document.

State of California

County of _____ } ss

On _____ , 20_____ , before me, _____ ,

personally appeared _____ , who proved to me on the basis of satisfactory evidence to be the person(s) whose name(s) is/are subscribed to the within instrument and acknowledged to me that he/she/they executed the same in his/her/their authorized capacity(ies), and that by his/her/their signature(s) on the instrument the person(s), or the entity upon behalf of which the person(s) acted, executed the instrument.

I certify under PENALTY OF PERJURY under the laws of the State of California that the foregoing paragraph is true and correct.

WITNESS my hand and official seal.

_____
Notary Public for the State of California

[NOTARY SEAL]   My commission expires _____

Notice of Revocation of Power of Attorney

I, _____ ,

of the City of _____ , County of _____ ,

State of California, revoke the power of attorney dated _____ ,

empowering _____

to act as my agent. I revoke and withdraw all power and authority granted under that power of attorney.

That power of attorney was recorded on _____ , _____ , with Instrument

Number _____ , in the Official Records, County of

_____ , State of California.

Dated: _____

_____
Signature of Principal

_____ , Principal

Certificate of Acknowledgment of Notary Public

A notary public or other officer completing this certificate verifies only the identity of the individual who signed the document to which this certificate is attached, and not the truthfulness, accuracy, or validity of that document.

State of California

County of _____ } ss

On _____ , 20 _____ , before me, _____ ,

personally appeared _____ , who

proved to me on the basis of satisfactory evidence to be the person(s) whose name(s) is/are subscribed to the within instrument and acknowledged to me that he/she/they executed the same in his/her/their authorized capacity(ies), and that by his/her/their signature(s) on the instrument the person(s), or the entity upon behalf of which the person(s) acted, executed the instrument.

I certify under PENALTY OF PERJURY under the laws of the State of California that the foregoing paragraph is true and correct.

WITNESS my hand and official seal.

_____
Notary Public for the State of California

[NOTARY SEAL]   My commission expires _____

Notice of Revocation of Power of Attorney

I, _____ ,

of the City of _____ , County of _____ ,

State of California, revoke the power of attorney dated _____ ,

empowering _____

to act as my agent. I revoke and withdraw all power and authority granted under that power of attorney.

Dated: _____

_____
Signature of Principal

_____ , Principal

Certificate of Acknowledgment of Notary Public

A notary public or other officer completing this certificate verifies only the identity of the individual who signed the document to which this certificate is attached, and not the truthfulness, accuracy, or validity of that document.

State of California ⎫
⎬ ss
County of _____ ⎭

On _____ , 20_____ , before me, _____ ,

personally appeared _____ , who proved to me on the basis of satisfactory evidence to be the person(s) whose name(s) is/are subscribed to the within instrument and acknowledged to me that he/she/they executed the same in his/her/their authorized capacity(ies), and that by his/her/their signature(s) on the instrument the person(s), or the entity upon behalf of which the person(s) acted, executed the instrument.

I certify under PENALTY OF PERJURY under the laws of the State of California that the foregoing paragraph is true and correct.

WITNESS my hand and official seal.

_____
Notary Public for the State of California

[NOTARY SEAL]   My commission expires _____

Index

A

Adoption, as power prohibited by law, 70

Advance health care directive, 1

 age requirement for, 18

 aid-in-dying as outside scope of, 8

 challenges to, prevention of, 20

 control of treatment retained, 19

 court invalidation of, 20–22

 distributing copies to appropriate persons, 46–47

 durable power of attorney for health care, 7, 26–29, 40–41

 duty of health care providers to honor, 18, 19–20, 26

 effective date of, delayed until doctor-determined incapacitation ("springing"), 18–19

 effective date of, immediate but not implemented until agent-determined incapacitation, 19

 effective date of, immediate implementation prior to incapacitation, 19

 Five Wishes document not recommended, 9

 form for, instructions for preparation of, 26–38, 46

 form for, sample, 39–45

 making your wishes known, 46–48

 MedicAlert bracelet or medallion to make wishes known, 9, 54

 mental capacity requirement, 11–12, 18, 20, 48

 notarization, 21, 38

 overview, 7–8, 18, 29

 reasons for planning ahead, 4–7, 12–13

 registration of, 46

 revoking, 20, 48–49

 signatures, 38, 46

 skilled nursing facility patients, witness required for, 46

 talking with appropriate persons, 47

 updating, 48

 wallet card for, 47

 witnesses, 21, 38, 46

 See also Advance health care directive, specifics of

Advance health care directive, specifics of

 artificial feeding and hydration, 31–32, 54

 blood transfusions, 30

 CPR (cardiopulmonary resuscitation), 30

 diagnostic tests, 30

 dialysis, 30

 drug treatments, 30

 final arrangements, 28

 instructions for receiving or withholding specific types of care, 32–34

 life-prolonging treatments or procedures, 29–31

 location of care, 35

 organ/tissue donation, 28, 36–37

 pain relief and palliative care, 31, 34–35

 personal or religious values, 35–36

 pregnancy, 21, 34

 primary physician, 37–38

 residence arrangements, 27

 respirator/ventilator use, 30–31

 surgery, 31

Agent

 multiple, issues involved with, 25, 76–77, 78, 90, 95, 100

 same person for health care and finance agents, as recommended, 10, 14, 25, 75, 76

 same person for many jobs, 75

Agent (finances)

 alternate (backup), 68, 74, 77–78, 80, 86–87, 88

appointment of, 10, 80

becoming unavailable, 102

as beneficiary, 83

choice of, factors to consider, 74–78

commingling of funds by, 72, 88

compensation and reimbursement of, 68, 78, 87–88

consent of agent candidate, 74

and death, termination of duties following, 68

delegation of authority by, 78, 88–89

expert help for, hiring of, 68, 73, 74

as fiduciary, 71, 96

geographical proximity of, 75

honesty and prudence of, 71–72

incapacitation determined by, as option, 61–62

incapacitation physician chosen by, 63, 87

keeping principal informed, 72

legal responsibilities of, 71–73

multiple agents, issues involved with, 76–77, 78, 90, 95, 100

nominated as conservator/guardian, 95

personal benefit of, 71–72, 88

power of, limits placed on, 60, 70, 80, 94

powers of, changing, 101–102

powers prohibited by law, 70

powers you can grant, 70, 80–86

record keeping by, 72–73

reporting/accountability, 73, 74, 94–95

resignations of (and breach of duty), 74

revoking authority of, 63, 73, 74, 101–105

as same person as health care agent, recommended, 10, 14, 25, 75, 76

special skills of, 71, 73

supervision of, 73–74, 94–95

trust for, as requirement, 61, 63, 74, 75, 95

will or living trust to allow continued authority of, 68

Agent (health care agent)

aid-in-dying not in scope of powers of, 8

alternate (backup), 7, 21, 26, 27, 28–29, 48

becoming unable to serve, 48

choice of, factors to consider, 24–25

contact information for, 27

copy of advance directive given to, 47–48

court invalidating authority of, 21–22

court permission sought to overrule your objections, 24

and death, final arrangements following, 15, 28

durable power of attorney naming, 7

form to designate, 26–29

geographical proximity of, 25

and immediate effect of advance directive, 19, 28

incapacitation determined by, as option, 8, 19

legal responsibilities of, 24

multiple agents, as not recommended, 25

need for, 22–23

persons prohibited by law to serve as, 25

powers, placing limits on, 7, 27–28

powers possible to grant, 23–24, 27–28

powers prohibited by law, 8, 24

residence arrangements by, 14, 27, 35

revoking authority of, 20, 48–49

as same person as finance agent, recommended, 10, 14, 25, 75, 76

when not to appoint, 7, 26

See also Advance health care directive

Aid-in-dying law, 8

Alzheimer's and other types of dementia, 13, 33, 35

Annuity and insurance transactions, 83

Antibiotics, 30, 54

Artificial feeding and hydration, 31–32, 54

Attorney-in-fact. *See* Agent (health care agent)

Attorney referral services, 109

Attorneys

for agent refusing to accept revocation, 102

for business operation by agent, 83

for challenges to advance directive, 20

for challenges to finance agent, 63, 70, 75

for durable power of attorney, 79, 83

for family conflicts, expectation of, 11, 12, 20

fees for, 108, 109

finding and working with, 108–109

for mental capacity requirement, 12
overview of need for, 12, 108
for review of durable power of attorney, 68
See also Legal document assistants
Autopsy, 15

B

Banking and other financial institutions
    check signing by agent, 82
    joint tenancy properties and need for durable
      power of attorney, 11
    power of attorney forms of, 82
    as power of finance agent, 82
    recording of power of attorney as reassurance
      for, 100
    safe deposit box for storing a springing
      durable power of attorney, not
      recommended, 101
    and spouse or domestic partner need for
      durable power of attorney, 10
Beneficiaries named by agent, 83
Bills, monthly, spouse/domestic partner paying,
  10
Blogs, as power of finance agent, 89–90
Blood transfusions, 30
Brokerage power of attorney forms, 81
Business operation
    agreements for, vs. power of attorney
      agreements, 70, 82–83
    and choice of agent, 74, 75, 77
    limitations on power of agent, 94
    as power of finance agent, 82–83, 94

C

California Durable Powers of Attorney
  (Continuing Education of the Bar), 110
California law
    changes in, revising advance directive
      according to, 48
    fraud/forgery of legal documents, 13
California Probate Code
    index to relevant sections of, 109
    law library research of, 110
    online legal research of, 110

overview, 4, 109
    statutory forms/short forms, 79
Caregiving
    coercion of loved ones, 13
    discussing need for planning with loved one,
      12–13
    online resources for, 13
    See also Conservatorships
Caretaking obligations, as power of finance
  agent, 85
Children (minors)
    care for, 14–15
    joint guardians for, 15
    maintenance of, as power of finance agent,
      84–85
Civil service benefits, 85
Claims, as finance agent power, 84
Coma, 30, 32, 33–34
Commodity and option transactions, 81
Computer access, as power of finance agent,
  89–90
Conservatorships
    advance directive and nomination of
      conservator, 28–29
    appropriate use of, 7, 11
    avoidance of, 6–7
    costs of, 68
    and court invalidation of power of attorney,
      68
    finance agent nominated as conservator, 95
    finance agent reporting and, 73, 74
    finance agent resignations and, 74
    finance agent turning over property and, 73
    online resources for, 13
    priority list for appointment of conservator,
      21–22
Contact information
    for agent, 27
    changes in, updating advance directive with,
      48
Corporations, finance agent and, 82–83
Courts
    agent seeking permission to make decision
      over your objections, 24, 72

compelling health care provider to honor advance care directive, 20

conservatorships and, 6–7, 21–22

for incapacitation finding, challenges to, 63

invalidation of advance directive, 20–21

invalidation of durable power of attorney for finances, 68, 95

revocation of agent's authority, 21–22, 74

supervision of finance agent by, 73–74

supervisory role an advantage if no appropriate agent available, 7, 11

CPR (cardiopulmonary resuscitation)

desire not to receive. *See* DNR form; DNR order; POLST form

explanation of, 30

D

Death

aid-in-dying law, 8

final arrangements following, 15, 16, 28

finances power of attorney terminating with, 68

health care agent and final arrangements following, 15, 28

termination of advance directive following, 22

Debt forgiveness by finance agent, 91

Dementia, 13, 33, 35

Diagnostic tests, 30

Dialysis, 30

Digital assets and accounts, as power of finance agent, 89–90

Disabilities, people with, and life support, 22–23

Divorce

and finances agent, 68, 76, 102

and health care agent, 22, 48

See also Domestic partnerships; Spouses

DNR form (Prehospital Do Not Resuscitate Form), 1

alerting appropriate persons of existence of, 54

alterations of, as invalidating, 54

copies of document, display of, 54

MedicAlert bracelet/medallion/membership, 9, 54

overview, 8–9, 52

POLST form compared to, 54

preparation of, 52

revoking, 54

sample form, 53

See also POLST form

DNR order, used in hospital medical records, 9

Domestic partnerships

and choice of finance agent, 75–76

and limits on persons eligible to serve as agent, 25

and need for durable power of attorney, 10

new registrations, 5

spousal rights granted to, 5

termination of, and revocation of finances agent, 68, 76, 102

termination of, and revocation of health care agent, 22, 48

Driver's license, organ donation and, 37

Drug treatments, 30

Durable power of attorney for finances

acceptance of, by institutions and government agencies, 69–70, 96

age requirement, 60

attorney help with, 79, 83

copies, distribution of, 101

cost and fees for, 68

court invalidation of, 68, 95

death as termination of, 68

defined, 10

determination of need for, 10–11

divorce or domestic partnership termination and, 68

effective date of, delayed until doctor-determined incapacitation ("springing"), 10, 62–63, 87, 101

effective date of, immediate but not implemented until agent-determined incapacitation, 10, 60–62, 100

effective date of, immediate implementation prior to incapacitation, 60

form, customized, 79

form for, as statutory, 79

form for, instructions for preparation of, 79–96, 100–101

form, sample, 97–99

incapacitation, finding of, 61–63

legalizing the document, 96–101

"living will" as term for, 5

lost document, 102

mental capacity requirement, 11–12, 60, 68, 70

name used on, legal and aka, 79–80

notarization of, 96, 100

overview, 1, 10–11, 60, 79–80

reasons for planning ahead, 4–7, 12–13

recording with county recorder's office, 68, 100, 104, 105

review with banks, insurers and other financial institutions, 96

revoking, 63, 74, 101–105

revoking, recording and notifying institutions of, 105

revoking, sample form for, 103–104

signatures for principal by, 82

signatures on form, 60, 96, 100

storage of signed document, 100–101

termination of, 63, 68

updating, 101, 102

See also Agent (finances); Durable power of attorney for finances, specifics of

Durable power of attorney for finances, specifics of

alternate agent, 86–87, 88

approval of others for actions of agent, 94

banking and financial institutions transactions, 82

beneficiary designations, 83

business operating transactions, 82–83, 94

civil or military service benefits, 85

claims and litigation, 84

commingling of funds by agent, 72, 88

commodity and option transactions, 81

compensation and reimbursement of agent, 87–88

conservator/guardian nomination, 95

delegation of duties by agent, 88–89

digital assets and accounts, access to, 89–90

effective date delayed until determination of incapacity ("springing"), 87

estate, trust, and other beneficiary transactions, 84

gifts to agent or others, 90–93

governmental benefits, 85

insurance and annuity transactions, 83

living trusts, creating/modifying/funding, 93–94

multiple agents, 90, 95

personal and family maintenance, 84–85

personal benefit by agent, 71–72, 88

personal property transactions, 81

pets, 85, 93

real property transactions, 81, 94

reporting/accountability, 94–95

retirement plan transactions, 85–86

social security benefits, 85

special instructions, 86–95

stock and bond transactions, 81

tax matters, 86

Durable power of attorney for health care, 7

as first part of advance directive form, 7

instructions for form, 26–29

sample form, 40–41

E

Email, as power of finance agent, 89–90

Emergency rooms, and DNR form, 9

Estate planning

by finance agent, 93–94

resources for, 16

See also Inheritance transactions; Living trusts; Wills

Estate taxes

gifts authorized by agent and, 91

online resource for status of, 91

F

Family members

conservatorships and, 6–7

copies of advance directive given to, 47

in disagreement about your wishes, 6

discussion about advance directive, 47

discussion about DNR form, 54

financial emergencies of, agent empowered to respond to, 91

maintenance of, as power of finance agent, 84–85

and reasons for planning ahead, 6

See also Caregiving; Children (minors); Family or third-party conflicts

Family or third-party conflicts

advance directive used to prevent, 20

attorney help in expectation of, 11, 12, 20

capacity requirement and, 12, 74

challenges to finance agent, 63, 70, 73–74, 75

conservatorship as preferable to durable power of attorney in case of, 11

durable power of attorney for finance and, 63, 95

incapacitation finding and, 62–63

likelihood of, and choice of agent, 25

need for agent and, 22–23

over living arrangements, 14

reporting requirement for finance agent and, 95

Feeding and hydration, artificial, 31–32, 54

Financial concerns, 36

Five Wishes advance directive, 9

Form books, legal research with, 110

Forms

cross-outs vs. erasures in, 79

customizing, 37, 38, 46, 79, 108

DNR form, obtaining, 52

downloadable, list of, 113

legal document assistant help with, 108

online location of, 112

PDFs, 112, 113

RTF form editing and managing, 112–113

statutory, 79

tear-out, use of, 26, 79

Friends

challenge to finance agent, 73–74

copy of advance directive given to, 47

talking with, about advance directive, 47

See also Family or third-party conflicts

Funeral arrangements, 15, 16, 37

G

Gifts to agent or others, 90–93

Gift taxes, 91, 92

Government benefits, 85

H

Health care agent. *See* Agent (health care agent)

Health care decisions

durable power of attorney for finances not empowered to make, 70

See also Advance health care directive

Health care providers

discussion of advance directive with, 47

duty to honor advance directive, 18, 19–20, 26

HIPAA release form, 23, 62, 64–66, 87

incapacitation finding by, 8, 18–19, 62–63, 87

as not eligible to serve as health care agents, 25

POLST form, assistance with, 57

and pregnancy, 21

receiving copy of advance directive, 46–47

transfer to doctor who will honor advance directive, 18, 19–20

verbal instructions to, for revocation of advance directive, 48–49

See also Hospital admissions; Primary physician

Health insurance company, copy of advance directive to, 47

HIPAA (Health Insurance Portability and Accountability Act), 23, 62

HIPAA release, 23, 62, 87

sample form, 64–66

Home, living arrangements outside of, 14, 27

Hospital admissions

DNR order placed in medical record, 9

and notarization of durable power of attorney, 100

preferred facility specified, 35

Hospital emergency rooms, honoring DNR forms, 9

Hydration and feeding, artificial, 31–32, 54

I

Incapacitation

advance directive effective upon, 8, 18–19

agent (finances) determination of, as option, 61–62

agent (health) determination of, as option, 8, 19

challenges to finding of, 63

defined, 18–19, 61

discussions of meaning of, 62, 63

doctor determination of, 8, 18–19, 62–63, 87

HIPAA release, 23, 62, 64–66, 87

naming doctor for determination of, 63, 87

one vs. two doctors for finding of, 63

Physician's Determination of Incapacity, 63, 67

reasons for planning for, 4–7

"springing" power of attorney for finances and determination of, 10, 61, 62–63, 87, 101

See also Mental capacity requirement

Inheritance transactions, 84

Institutions

acceptance of durable power of attorney for finances, 69–70, 96

naming as agent, as not recommended, 77

Insurance and annuity transactions, 83

IRS power of attorney form, 86

J

Joint guardians, 15

Joint tenancy property

and need for durable power of attorney, 11

and personal benefit clause for agent, 72

L

Lawsuits, as finance agent power, 84

Lawyers. See Attorneys

LDAs (legal document assistants), 108

Legal document assistants (LDAs), 108

Legal research, 109–110

MP3 information files from Nolo, 112, 113

Life-prolonging treatments or procedures

advance directive addressing, 29–31

exceptions to directive, 32–34

Limited liability companies, finance agent and, 82–83

Litigation, as finance agent power, 84

Living trusts

benefits of, 84

for durable power of attorney continuing after death, 68

finance agent creating/modifying/revoking/ funding, 84, 93–94

finance agent turning over property to, 73

and need for durable power of attorney, 10

powers of successor trustee for, vs. power of attorney for finances, 70

successor trustee of, as same person as other agents, 75, 76

as transfer method, 15

transfers of property to, as power of finance agent, 84, 93–94

Living will. See Advance health care directive

Loan forgiveness by finance agent, 91

Long-term care, 13–14, 35

employees/operators of facilities not eligible to be agent, 25

witness requirements for patients in skilled nursing facilities, 46

M

Marriage

as power of agent prohibited by law, 70

See also Divorce; Domestic partnerships; Spouses

Medicaid benefits, 85

MedicAlert bracelet/medallion/membership, 9, 54

Medical personnel. See Health care providers

Medicare benefits, 85

Memorial services, 16

Mental capacity requirement

for advance health care directive, 11–12, 18, 20, 48

for durable power of attorney, 11–12, 60, 68, 70

Military service benefits, 85

MP3 information files from Nolo, 112, 113

N

Name, legal and aka, 79–80

Nolo Lawyer Directory, 108–109

Notarization

of advance health care directive, 21, 38

of durable power of attorney, 96, 100

of revocation of durable power of attorney, 102

O

Online accounts, as power of finance agent, 89–90

Online resources

artificial nutrition and hydration, 32

attorney directory, 108–109

caregiver support, 13

conservatorship, 13

digital assets and accounts, status of law regarding, 89

DNR form, obtaining, 52

domestic partnership registration, 5

estate planning, 16

estate tax changes, 91

Five Wishes document, 9

forms and worksheets, 2, 112

legal research, 110

MedicAlert bracelet/medallion/membership, 54

organ donation, 36, 37

palliative care, 35

POLST form, 57

professional fiduciaries as agent, 77

registration of advance directive, 46

religions' views on organ donation, 36

Social Security representative payee, 85

Option and commodity transactions, 81

Organs, tissue, and body part donations, 8, 28, 36–37

P

Pain management and palliative care, 31, 34–35

Palliative care/pain relief, 31, 34–35

Parents, care of minor children, 14–15

Partnerships (business), finance agent and, 70, 82–83

PDF forms, 112

Personal property. *See* Property; Real estate

Pets, finance agent and, 85, 93

Physician-assisted suicide. *See* Aid-in-dying law

Physician Orders for Life-Sustaining Treatment. *See* POLST form

Physician's Determination of Incapacity, 63
sample form, 67

Physicians. *See* Health care providers; Primary physician

POLST form (Physician Orders for Life-Sustaining Treatment), 1, 9

DNR form compared to, 54

health care providers assisting with, 57

online resource for, 57

overview, 52, 54

sample form, 55–56

signatures required for, 54

See also DNR form

Power of attorney

brokerage house forms for, 81

defined, 7

financial institution forms for, 82, 96

IRS form for, 86

nondurable, 7

See also Durable power of attorney for finances; Durable power of attorney for health care

Pregnancy, 21, 34

Primary physician

advance directive naming, 8, 37–38

copy of advance directive to, 46–47

copy of DNR form to, 54

discussion of advance directive with, 47

durable power of attorney for finances
naming, 87
and HIPAA release form, 23, 62, 64–66, 87
incapacitation as determined by, 8, 18–19,
62–63, 87
signature on DNR form required, 52
and verbal instructions to revoke advance
directive, 48–49
and verbal instructions to revoke authority of
agent, 49
See also Health care providers
Probate, avoidance of, 15
Property
of children, management specified in will, 15
finance agent turning over, 73
joint tenancy, and need for power of attorney,
11
and living trust (successor trustee) need for
durable power of attorney, 10
as power of finance agent, 81–82
and spouse's or domestic partner's need for
power of attorney, 10
See also Real estate

R

Real estate
as joint tenancy, and need for durable power
of attorney, 11
limitations on power of agent, 94
as power of finance agent, 81, 94
recording finance agent with county clerk,
68, 100, 105
and spouse or domestic partner need for
durable power of attorney, 10
Record keeping by agent, 72–73
Records, consistency of name used on, 80
Religion
and advance directive form, 35–36
and organ donation, 36
Reporting/accountability by finance agent, 73,
74, 94–95
Request to Forgo Resuscitative Measures. See
DNR form (Prehospital Do Not Resuscitate
Form)

Residence
change of, revoking durable power of
attorney for, 102
decisions for receiving care in, 14, 27, 35
updating changes of, 48
Respirator/ventilator use, 30–31
Retirement plan transactions, 85–86
RTF forms, 112

S

Safe deposit box not recommended for storage
of durable power of attorney, 101
Same-sex partners. See Domestic partnerships;
Spouses; Unmarried couples
Skilled nursing facilities, witness signature on
advance directive for patients in, 46
Social media accounts, as power of finance
agent, 89–90
Social Security Administration contact
information, 85
Social Security checks and benefits, 85
Sole proprietorships, finance agent and, 82–83
"Sound mind". See Mental capacity requirement
Spiritual beliefs or traditions, 35–36
Spouses
divorce of, 22, 48, 68, 76, 102
as finance agent, 75–76, 102
finance agent turning over property to, 73
marriage as power of agent prohibited by law,
70
and need for durable power of attorney, 10
See also Domestic partnerships; Unmarried
couples
Stock and bond transactions, 81
Surgery, 31

T

Tax matters, as power of finance agent, 86
See also Estate taxes; Gift taxes
Terminal illness, directive for, 33
Third-party conflicts. See Family or third-party
conflicts

U

Unmarried couples, and need for planning ahead, 5

U.S. Supreme Court
right to control one's medical care, 18
strong evidence of wishes for care to be honored, 21

V

Ventilator/respirator use, 30–31
Voting, as power prohibited by law, 70

W

Wallet card, 47

Wills
beneficiaries of, finance agent changing, 93
children, care of minor, 15
children's property, management of, 15
for durable power of attorney continuing after death, 68
personal representative (executor), as same person as other agents, 75
as power of finance agent prohibited by law, 70, 93
property disposition, 15
See also Living trusts

NOLO *Save 15% off your next order*

Register your Nolo purchase, and we'll send you a **coupon for 15% off** your next Nolo.com order!

Nolo.com/customer-support/productregistration

On Nolo.com you'll also find:

Books & Software
Nolo publishes hundreds of great books and software programs for consumers and business owners. Order a copy, or download an ebook version instantly, at Nolo.com.

Online Legal Documents
You can quickly and easily make a will or living trust, form an LLC or corporation, apply for a trademark or provisional patent, or make hundreds of other forms—online.

Free Legal Information
Thousands of articles answer common questions about everyday legal issues including wills, bankruptcy, small business formation, divorce, patents, employment, and much more.

Plain-English Legal Dictionary
Stumped by jargon? Look it up in America's most up-to-date source for definitions of legal terms, free at nolo.com.

Lawyer Directory
Nolo's consumer-friendly lawyer directory provides in-depth profiles of lawyers all over America. You'll find all the information you need to choose the right lawyer.

CPOA5